Sports Illustrated
FOR KIDS

Aleen

INSIDER'S GUIDE TO ACTION SPORTS

BY MATT HIGGINS

SCHOLASTIC REFERENCE

AN IMPRINT OF

SCHOLASTIC

Cover photography credit: Pete Demos/Haro Bikes
Back-cover photography credits: Bob Burnquist by Atiba Jefferson, Gretchen Bleiler by Mark Gallup

SPORTS ILLUSTRATED FOR KIDS: Insider's Guide to Action Sports is a production of SPORTS ILLUSTRATED FOR KIDS: Neil Cohen, Managing Editor; Erin Egan, Senior Editor/Editorial Projects; Ellen Labrecque, Senior Editor; Matt Higgins, Author; Edward Duarte, Designer; Ryan Schick, Photo Editor; Davin Coburn, Reporter.

Scholastic Reference staff: Kenneth Wright, Editorial Director; Mary Varilla Jones, Senior Editor; Brenda Murray, Assistant Editor; Karyn Browne, Managing Editor; Melinda Weigel, Production Editor; Becky Terhune, Art Director; Jess White, Manufacturing Coordinator.

Acknowledgments
The author would like to thank those people who shared their time and expertise in making the *Insider's Guide to Action Sports* possible: Erin Egan, Ellen Labrecque, and Neil Cohen for ensuring that this project hewed to its original design; Loren Anderson, Ed Klim, Mark Larsen, and Scott O'Malley for quick, but thorough lessons in snowmobiles and snowmobile racing; Arlo Eisenberg and Chris Mitchell for enthusiastic first-hand accounts of every step in aggressive inline's young history; Kevin Michael for his encyclopedic knowledge of wakeboarding; Patrick Wampler for taking the time to explain stuff; and finally, to Keith Mulligan for always responding to BMX questions. Just in case I've forgotten anyone, thanks to you, too!

CONTENTS

CHAPTER 1

BMX

In the 1970's, bicycle motocross riders took
the sport from dirt tracks into the air.

Dave Mirra has won the
most medals (19) in the
history of the X Games.

MARK LOSEY

The velocipede, the first bicycle with pedals, was invented in 1863. It was made of iron with a stiff, uncomfortable saddle seat, a straight handlebar, and large metal wheels. It would be 100 years before the first BMX bike appeared.

By the mid-1940's, bikes became cheaper to make. For the first time, most parents could afford to buy them for their kids. In 1963, Schwinn, a bike company, experimented with motorcycle-style designs and came up with the Sting-Ray. The Sting-Ray had 20-inch wheels, which were smaller than the wheels of other bikes at the time. This popular model handled and turned better, allowing riders to do simple tricks, such as wheelies.

BMX Is Born

At the same time, motocross racing was getting hot in the United States. Because the Sting-Ray looked like a motorcycle, kids copied the moves of their favorite motocross riders on their bikes. Bike riders in Los Angeles, California, soon began racing around dirt tracks, and a sport was born. It was called bicycle motocross, but eventually it was shortened to BMX.

In 1973, the first true BMX bike was created when Schwinn modified the Sting-Ray by moving the wheels farther apart and making the crank (the wheel that moves the chain) larger. These changes gave the bike more stability and speed.

Riding High

In 1974, the first national BMX race, the Yamaha Gold Cup, was held in Van Nuys, California. In 1975, a company called BMX Products introduced the first aluminum wheel. The wheel, called the Motomag, was sturdy enough to take the punishment of BMX riding. Publications devoted to the new sport began. The first was *Bicycle Motocross News*. Another, *Bicycle Motocross Action*, began publishing in 1976.

By the mid-1970's, some BMX riders were taking the sport in a new direction. A group of bikers in Southern California were riding in empty swimming pools, much like what skateboarders were doing at the time.

Ryan Nyquist is a double threat in park and dirt.

MARK LOSEY

Other riders were pulling aerials and tricks in the new skateparks of Southern California. In its October 1975 issue, *BMX Weekly* ran a photo of Stu Thomsen, a BMX racer, doing a 360 aerial. By late 1977, Thomsen was flying higher. A picture of him on his bike doing a one-handed air at the SkaterCross Skateboard Park in Reseda, California, was the first published photo of an aerial on vert. The photo appeared in an ad in the April 1978 issue of *Bicycle Motocross News*. It helped change the direction of BMX from racing to what would be known as Freestyle.

The First Freestylers

Freestyle would grow into five distinct disciplines: vert, street, park, dirt, and flatland. Riders pulled tricks in all of the disciplines. Vert riders performed on ramps and in pools. Street riders used the natural terrain and

Morgan Wade is known for his huge tricks and spectacular spills.

obstacles of the street. Park riders did their stuff on ramps and jumps in skateparks. Dirt riders rolled over a series of dirt jumps. Flatland riders performed on any hard, level surface, such as a parking lot or driveway.

Bob Haro is considered the father of Freestyle riding. He worked as a staff artist for *Bicycle Motocross Action* magazine. During his lunch breaks, Haro would ride his bike in the parking lot outside the magazine's Southern California office. Photos of those sessions soon appeared in the magazine. The first trick featured was the rock walk, in which Haro rotated his bike's tires in a walking motion across the parking lot.

Spreading the Sport

By 1979, *Bicycle Motocross Action* formed a team to tour the country and perform tricks. On the team with Haro was R.L. Osborne, whose father, Bob, was the publisher of *Bicycle Motocross Action*. Haro and Osborne introduced Freestyle to kids all over the country, increasing the popularity of the sport.

By 1984, new equipment allowed Freestyle to surge past BMX racing in popularity. Steve Potts, a bike builder, invented the Potts Mod, which allowed handlebars to spin without tangling the front brake cables. Early versions of pegs appeared. Pegs screw onto the end of

wheel axles and allow riders to stand on them. They opened the door to a whole new range of tricks.

Rolling Along

BMX Freestyle, which eventually became *Freestylin'*, began publishing in 1984. It was the first magazine just for Freestyle riding. Tricks progressed, too. Jose Yanez pulled the first backflip and Josh White pulled the first 540 that year. The following year, the National Freestyle Association was founded.

In 1986, BMX bike company Skyway sponsored a 14-year-old phenom from Edmond, Oklahoma, named Mat Hoffman. He would go on to win 10 world championships during his career.

BMX had hit the mainstream by the mid-1980's. A 1985 Mountain Dew TV commercial featured top Freestylers Ron Wilkerson, Eddie Fiola, and R.L. Osborne riding their bikes. A movie about BMX racing, *Rad*, opened in 1986. But things soon took a turn for the worse.

Bump in the Road

Mountain biking grew in popularity in 1989, and BMX took a backseat. BMX competitions were rare, but die-hard riders kept at it. Hoffman, in particular, pushed the progression of BMX by trying more difficult tricks. He pulled the first 900 (2 ½-rotations) at a King of Vert contest in Toronto, Ontario, Canada, in 1989. In 1990, he nailed the first flair (a backflip with a 180-degree spin) and the first flip fakie (a backflip, landing backward). Hoffman's next and most challenging trick: make BMX popular again. To do so, he founded the Bicycle Stunt Series, with competitions for street, ramp, and flatland.

Hoffman's involvement in the business of Freestyle BMX increased its visibility. Another big aid to promoting the sport arrived in 1995, when the first X Games were held in Providence, Rhode Island. (They were first called the Extreme Games but changed to the X Games in 1996.)

Hoffman won the X Games gold medal in Vert in 1995 and Jay Miron won gold in Dirt. Street was added in 1996 and Flatland in 1997.

Mirra's Arrival

A talented young rider named Dave Mirra soon became the dominant vert and park rider of the next 10 years. Mirra is known for getting huge air and making the hardest tricks look simple. He has won a total of 19 X Games medals, including 14 gold.

By 2001, Hoffman's competitive career was winding down. But he still strove to make a lasting mark on the sport. He built a 24-foot-tall quarterpipe ramp and flew 26 feet above it. Soaring 50 feet above the ground, he set a Guinness World Record for height on a BMX bike.

Stars of Today

Ryan Nyquist emerged as a star in park and dirt. He won an X Games medal in Dirt every year from 1997 through 2003. Lately, several top international riders have begun to contend for medals. Jamie Bestwick of England won his third gold medal in Vert at the 2005 X Games. A crew of Australians, led by Ryan Guettler, has soared to the top in dirt and park.

In 40 years, the sport of BMX has come full circle. Originally inspired by motocross during the 1960's, it is now a sport all its own. Today, its influence is apparent when Freestyle motocross riders pull tricks high in the air *(see Chapter 3)*.

INNOVATOR

JAMIE BESTWICK

Jamie Bestwick visited Camp Woodward in Woodward, Pennsylvania, in the summer of 1998. At the time, the 6' 1" Englishman was working as an engineer in an aeronautics factory in Nottingham, England. Bike stunt riding was just a hobby for him. But after his trip, Bestwick decided to make riding a full-time gig. In 1999, he quit his job, sold his house, and moved to a town near Camp Woodward. He rode nearly every day. Bestwick soon went from a little-known rider with a British accent to a bike-stunt star. He won the gold medal in Vert at the 1999 Gravity Games. In 2000, he won gold in Vert at the X Games. At the 2003 Global X Games, Bestwick pulled the first tailwhip flair in competition. The trick requires the rider to flip backward and spin 180 degrees while rotating the back of his bike 360 degrees. In 2005, Bestwick began pulling double tailwhip flairs. If he hadn't moved to the United States in 1999, Bestwick might still be working in an airplane parts factory. Instead, his career has taken flight.

K oji Kraft grew up riding near Chicago, Illinois. He began competing in Vert at an Asian X Games qualifier in 2000. Ever since, Kraft has been known for pulling tricks high above the ramp. He also has sick mini-ramp skills and won the event at the 2005 UCI BMX World Championships. On the big ramp, Kraft's best result was sixth at the 2005 Gravity Games. At age 23, he is still one of the youngest vert riders competing today. Kraft is expected to crack the Top 5 at major events in the near future.

FAST FACT

A gyro is a part of the braking system located where the handlebars meet the frame of the bike. A gyro is one of the most important innovations in the development of Freestyle BMX. It allows the handlebars to spin around without tangling the brake cables. With a gyro, a rider can do tricks such as bar spins and tailwhips.

<GREATEST MOMENT>
MAT HOFFMAN'S HEIGHT RECORD

egend Mat Hoffman has always tried to go as high as possible on his bike. In 1999, he even rode off a 3,500-foot-tall cliff in Norway with a parachute strapped to his back. Hoffman began chasing big air records during the early 1990's. In 1992, he built a 21-foot-tall quarterpipe and soared 20 feet above it. Two years later, he topped 23 feet. (Neither mark was a certified Guinness World Record.) Then in 1999, Hoffman Bikes team member Kevin Robinson set the official Guinness World Record for height on a bike, reaching 15 feet, 3 inches above a ramp. In 2001, Dave Mirra beat Robinson's record with a 19-foot air. Later that same year, Hoffman put the record out of reach. He cleared more than 26 feet on a 24-foot-tall quarterpipe. In 2004, Guinness officially recognized Hoffman's huge air as the world record. No one has surpassed the height since.

MICHAEL CASTILLO/HOFFMAN ENTERPRISES

NECESSARY OBJECTS

- **BIKE:** Most BMX bikes come with 20-inch tires and a basic frame, whether you're racing or performing Freestyle tricks. BMX racing bikes are stripped-down versions of BMX bikes, which makes them faster. Racing bikes don't come with pegs, a gyro (a part in the braking system that allows the handlebars to spin around without tangling brake cables), or front brakes. Racing tires are also knobbier, offering better traction in the dirt.

  BMX dirt-jumping bikes are similar to racing bikes. They don't have pegs, a gyro, or front brakes. They need tires with good tread. Dirt-jumping bikes must be durable because they take a beating.

  BMX Freestyle bikes (street, park, and vert) also have to be tough enough to take a lot of abuse. They tend to be heavier because of the pegs, gyro, and front brakes. These accessories help riders pull tricks. The tires don't need much tread because the bikes are ridden mostly on concrete.

  Flatland bikes vary in design, depending on style and personal preferences. The frames tend to be smaller than the frames for bikes in the other disciplines. Flatland bikes should have four pegs (two on each wheel), a gyro, and front and rear brakes. These extras help the rider perform highly technical tricks. Like Freestyle bikes, the tires on flatland bikes have little tread. Although it's possible to ride flatland on a Freestyle bike, it's difficult to ride Freestyle on a flatland bike. Beginners should stick with a Freestyle setup before they decide to specialize. All BMX bikes, no matter what discipline, can be custom built from parts at a local bike store. But beginners will find that a preassembled bike offers everything they need.

- **HELMET:** A skate helmet will protect your head from injury for flatland and most Freestyle riding. Riders should wear a helmet rated by the U.S. Consumer Product Safety Commission (CPSC). Racers and advanced Freestyle trick riders wear a motorcycle-style helmet with a full face shield for better protection. Most skateparks and racing leagues require that riders wear some type of helmet.

- **PADS:** A basic set of skate pads covers knees and elbows. It may look as though Freestyle riders aren't wearing knee pads, but they are. The style is to wear them underneath a pair of pants. Some top pros, including Jamie Bestwick, also wear shin guards. Most skateparks insist that riders wear some padding.

ME LINE

COURTESY OF SCHWINN

e Sting-Ray

BMX

1963 Schwinn manufactures the Sting-Ray, the first BMX bike.

1971 Bruce Brown's film, *On Any Sunday*, showcases BMX to national audiences, spurring interest in the new sport.

1974 *Bicycle Motocross News*, the first national magazine to cover BMX racing, begins publishing

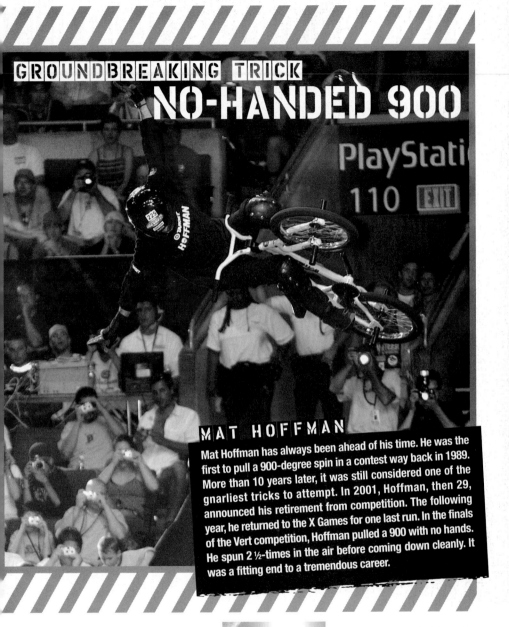

NO-HANDED 900

PlayStati

110 EXIT

MAT HOFFMAN

Mat Hoffman has always been ahead of his time. He was the first to pull a 900-degree spin in a contest way back in 1989. More than 10 years later, it was still considered one of the gnarliest tricks to attempt. In 2001, Hoffman, then 29, announced his retirement from competition. The following year, he returned to the X Games for one last run. In the finals of the Vert competition, Hoffman pulled a 900 with no hands. He spun 2 ½-times in the air before coming down cleanly. It was a fitting end to a tremendous career.

975 Bikers begin ~ving in empty pools Southern California.

1976 Carlsbad Skatepark, the first skatepark in California, opens. It lets BMX riders use the facility.

Bob Haro

JAMES CASSIMUS

1979 A photo of Bob Haro performing the rock walk, the first true Freestyle BMX trick, appears in the January/February issue of *Bicycle Motocross Action*.

THE BASIC TRICKS

BUNNY HOP▶

The bunny hop is an aerial on a bike. It's as basic as the wheelie. The trick requires the rider to roll forward at a normal speed, level the pedals, lean backward, and pull up on the handlebars. This will raise the front tire off the ground. Next, the rider lifts his knees to allow the back wheel to come off the ground, too. Once in the air, he levels the tires so they will come down evenly on the ground. The rider can bunny hop over curbs and other obstacles.

MARK LOSEY

MARK LOSEY

◀BAR SPIN

Bar spins should be practiced on the ground before trying to do them in the air. The rider should start with his left hand backward on the grip and his right hand facing forward. While rolling forward on the bike, he spins the handlebars clockwise 180 degrees. The turn is done quickly. Once he has it down, the rider can move on to 360-degree bar spins on flat ground or 180s off a curb or small ramp.

TIME LINE

1981 Bob Morales and Eddie Fiola start the Amateur Skatepark Association (ASPA). ASPA promotes skatepark-style Freestyle riding and offers cash prizes, leading to the first Freestyle pro divisions.

E.T. gets a BMX ride.

UNIVERSAL/EVERETT COLLECTION

1982 The movie *E.T. — The Extra-Terrestrial* features kids riding BMX bikes.

1988 The Freestyl video *Dork in York 2* debuts. It features a 13-year-old h shot named Dave Mirra.

CAN-CAN▶

Can-cans require getting air. The rider launches off a ramp and kicks either his left or right foot — whichever feels more comfortable — over to the opposite side of the bike. The other foot stays on the pedal. After mastering the can-can, the next step is the no-footed can-can. The trick requires the rider to remove both feet from the pedals. It was invented by rider Mike Dominguez in 1986.

CARLETON HALL/AMID/ICON SMI

F🅰S🆃 FACT

A superman is an advanced trick that requires the rider to fly through the air. He extends his body horizontally with both feet dangling off the back of the bike, while holding the handlebars with one hand. Rider Bob Kohl pulled the first one in 1987.

992 *Ride* magazine begins publishing in the United States.

1994 Dave Mirra joins the Haro team.

The X Games

MATT YORK/AP

1995 The first X Games (then called the Extreme Games) debut in Providence, Rhode Island. Mat Hoffman wins gold in Vert and Jay Miron wins gold in Dirt.

< U P – A N D – C O M E R >
CHAD KAGY

Chad Kagy, age 28, is a veteran in street and park. He won the bronze medal in Street at the 1999 X Games and in Park at the 2002 Games. But he has transformed himself into a rising vert star. He lives near Camp Woodward in Pennsylvania and rides daily with vert masters Jamie Bestwick and Kevin Robinson. Kagy suffered a serious setback when he broke his neck while riding in September 2003. But he worked hard to return to form and was back on his bike the next year. Kagy won the silver medal in Vert at the 2005 X Games. He also captured bronze in Vert Best Trick with a flatspin flair tailwhip.

MARK LOSEY

FAST FACT
A badly bent wheel is called a *potato chip*.

TIME LINE

1997 Jay Miron pulls the first 540 tailwhip.

Jay Miron

SHAZAM!/ESPN IMAGES

2000 Mike "Rooftop" Escamilla jumps over a helicopter with its blades running on a television show for MTV. He later flips over the helicopter with its blades still.

< LEGEND >
MAT HOFFMAN

Mat Hoffman's nickname is "The Condor" because he reaches great heights on his bike. He is responsible for pushing BMX vert to new levels. Hoffman has invented more than 100 tricks during his career, including the flair (a backflip with a 180-degree spin) and flip fakie (a backflip, landing backward). His skills as a businessman also helped the young sport survive through rough times.

Hoffman turned pro in Freestyle BMX at age 16. He soon became the top vert rider due to his creativity and his willingness to attempt high-flying airs. Hoffman won the world championship 10 times from 1987 through 1996. During that stretch, he went three years without losing a competition. Hoffman also won the gold medal in Vert at the first two X Games (1995 and 1996). But BMX was losing kids to the hot, new sport of mountain biking.

To help BMX rebound, Hoffman started his own team of Freestyle riders, the Sprocket Jockey Bicycle Stunt Team. Hoffman's team toured the country, performing demonstrations. He also created his own company, Hoffman Bikes, in 1991. Hoffman bikes were sturdier and could stand up to the pounding of Freestyle better than other bikes on the market. He also began two competition series and founded the Hoffman Sports Association, a worldwide sanctioning body for Freestyle BMX.

Today, Hoffman is almost as well-known for his slams as he is for his success. He has had more than a dozen operations. Now 34 years old, The Condor has retired from competition. He still performs from time to time, however, most notably with Tony Hawk's Boom Boom HuckJam tour.

MICHAEL CASTILLO/HOFFMAN ENTERPRISES

2001 Mat Hoffman soars 26 feet above a 24-foot-tall ramp for a total of 50 feet, a world record for height on a bike.

2003 Ryan Nyquist wins gold in Park and Dirt at the X Games.

Ryan Nyquist

BAKKE/SHAZAMM/ESPN IMAGES

2005 The documentary *Joe Kid on a Sting-Ray* is released. It tells the history of BMX.

DOUBLE BACKFLIP

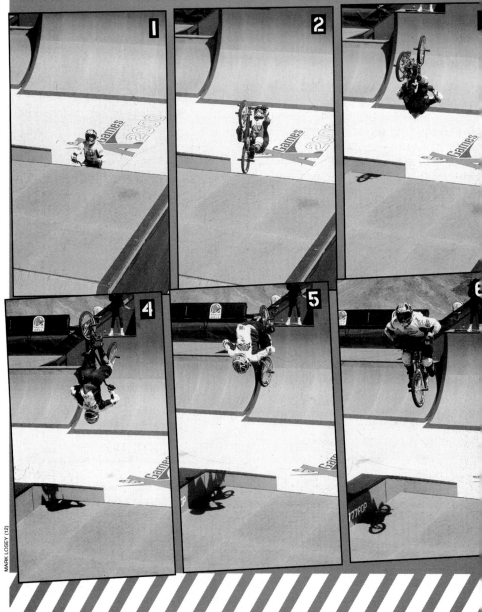

MARK LOSEY (12)

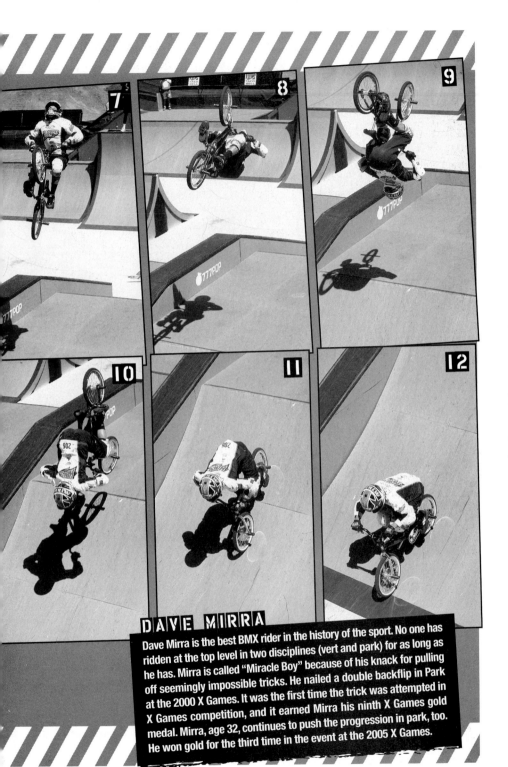

DAVE MIRRA

Dave Mirra is the best BMX rider in the history of the sport. No one has ridden at the top level in two disciplines (vert and park) for as long as he has. Mirra is called "Miracle Boy" because of his knack for pulling off seemingly impossible tricks. He nailed a double backflip in Park at the 2000 X Games. It was the first time the trick was attempted in X Games competition, and it earned Mirra his ninth X Games gold medal. Mirra, age 32, continues to push the progression in park, too. He won gold for the third time in the event at the 2005 X Games.

TOP 10 ATHLETES

1 DAVE MIRRA, born April 4, 1974, in Syracuse, New York. Mirra is the greatest Freestyle bike rider in the sport's history. He has won more medals (19) than any athlete in X Games history, including 14 gold. Miracle Boy flies higher on runs than any other rider. At age 32, he is still a master in vert and park.

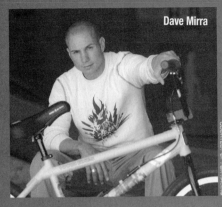

Dave Mirra

2 RYAN NYQUIST, born March 6, 1979, in Los Gatos, California. Nyquist rules dirt and park. He won gold in both at the 2003 X Games. In 2005, Nyquist finished third in Park at the X Games and on the inaugural Dew Action Sports Tour.

3 JAMIE BESTWICK, born July 8, 1971, in Nottingham, England. Bestwick and Dave Mirra are neck and neck for the top spot in vert. Bestwick has won six X Games medals, including five gold. In 2005, he won gold in Vert and Vert Best Trick at the X Games, Vert at the Gravity Games, and the Vert title on the Dew Action Sports Tour.

Jamie Bestwick

4 RYAN GUETTLER, born July 17, 1983, in Brisbane, Australia. Guettler won the bronze medal in Park at the 2004 X Games. In 2005, he had the best year of his career. He won gold at the Gravity Games and bronze at the X Games, both in Dirt. He also won Park and Dirt titles on the 2005 Dew Action Sports Tour.

5 CHAD KAGY, born November 21, 1978, in Gilroy, California. Kagy used to spread his talents between dirt and park. He now excels in vert. In 2005, he won the silver medal in Vert and the bronze medal in Vert Best Trick at the X Games. Kagy also finished third in Vert on the Dew Action Sports Tour.

Chad Kagy

6 KEVIN ROBINSON, born December 19, 1971, in East Providence, Rhode Island. This vert veteran is known for performing his no-handed flair and for inventing the corkscrew (a backflip with a twist). Robinson has won four X Games medals in Vert, including bronze in 2005. He also placed second in Vert on the 2005 Dew Action Sports Tour.

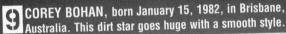

Kevin Robinson

CHRISTIAN PONDELLA

7 MIKE ESCAMILLA, born August 8, 1977, in La Habra, California. Escamilla's nickname is "Rooftop." He is one of the first riders to jump from one rooftop to another. He is a pioneer in street riding. Many other riders have tried to copy his tricks, but the stunts are just too gnarly. In 2005, he set two Guinness World Records on the Mega Ramp, which is used at the X Games. He launched a backflip 62 feet, 2 inches high and spun a one-handed tabletop 360 — something that had never been attempted.

JEFF ZIELINSKI

Mike Escamilla

8 MAT HOFFMAN, born January 9, 1972, in Edmond, Oklahoma. Hoffman has risen higher and slammed harder than anyone in BMX vert. The Condor won 10 world titles from 1987 through 1996. He won six X Games medals in Vert, including two gold medals. Hoffman stopped competing in 2002, but could still be one of the top riders if he returned today.

9 COREY BOHAN, born January 15, 1982, in Brisbane, Australia. This dirt star goes huge with a smooth style. He won the silver medal in Dirt at the 2003 X Games. Bohan followed that with the gold medal at the 2004 X Games, knocking off defending champ Ryan Nyquist. In 2005, Bohan repeated as X Games Dirt champ and placed second in the event on the Dew Action Sports Tour.

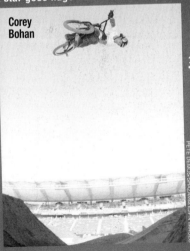

Corey Bohan

PETE DEMOS/SHAZAMM/ESPN IMAGES

10 DENNIS McCOY, born December 29, 1966, in Kansas City, Missouri. This 39-year-old is a legend who has ridden every discipline over the years. McCoy has 20 years of pro experience and still brings it. He won the year-end BMX Freestyle title from 1986-95. McCoy also has five X Games medals to his credit. In 2005, he won the silver medal in Vert at the Gravity Games.

X GAMES RESULTS

YEAR	EVENT	GOLD	SILVER	BRONZE
2005	Dirt	Corey Bohan, Australia	Chris Doyle, U.S.	Ryan Guettler, Australia
2004	Dirt	Corey Bohan, Australia	Chris Doyle, U.S.	T.J. Lavin, U.S.
2003	Dirt	Ryan Nyquist, U.S.	Corey Bohan, Australia	Chris Doyle, U.S.
2002	Dirt	Allan Cooke, U.S.	Ryan Nyquist, U.S.	Chris Doyle, U.S.
2001	Dirt	Stephen Murray, Great Britain	Ryan Nyquist, U.S.	T.J. Lavin, U.S.
2000	Dirt	Ryan Nyquist, U.S.	Cory Nastazio, U.S.	T.J. Lavin, U.S.
1999	Dirt	T.J. Lavin, U.S.	Brian Foster, U.S.	Ryan Nyquist, U.S.
1998	Dirt	Brian Foster, U.S.	Ryan Nyquist, U.S.	Joey Garcia, U.S.
1997	Dirt	T.J. Lavin, U.S.	Brian Foster, U.S.	Ryan Nyquist, U.S.
1996	Dirt	Joey Garcia, U.S.	T.J. Lavin, U.S.	Brian Foster, U.S.
1995	Dirt	Jay Miron, Canada	Taj Mihelich, U.S.	Joey Garcia, U.S.
2003	Flatland	Simon O'Brien, Australia	Nathan Penonzek, Canada	Trevor Meyer, U.S.
2002	Flatland	Martti Kuoppa, Finland	Michael Steingraeber, Germany	Phil Dolan, Great Britain
2001	Flatland	Martti Kuoppa, Finland	Phil Dolan, Great Britain	Matt Wilhelm, U.S.
2000	Flatland	Martti Kuoppa, Finland	Michael Steingraeber, Germany	Phil Dolan, Great Britain
1999	Flatland	Trevor Meyer, U.S.	Phil Dolan, Great Britain	Nathan Penonzek, Canada
1998	Flatland	Trevor Meyer, U.S.	Andrew Faris, Canada	Martti Kuoppa, Finland
1997	Flatland	Trevor Meyer, U.S.	Nate Hanson, U.S.	Andrew Faris, Canada
2005	Park	Dave Mirra, U.S.	Scotty Cranmer, U.S.	Ryan Nyquist, U.S.
2004	Park	Dave Mirra, U.S.	Ryan Nyquist, U.S.	Ryan Guettler, Australia
2003	Park	Ryan Nyquist, U.S.	Gary Young, U.S.	Dave Mirra, U.S.
2002	Park	Ryan Nyquist, U.S.	Alistair Whitton, Great Britain	Chad Kagy, U.S.
2001	Park	Bruce Crisman, U.S.	Alistair Whitton, Great Britain	Jay Miron, Canada
2000	Park	Dave Mirra, U.S.	Markus Wilke, Germany	Ryan Nyquist, U.S.
1999	Street	Dave Mirra, U.S.	Jay Miron, Canada	Chad Kagy, U.S.
1998	Street	Dave Mirra, U.S.	Jay Miron, Canada	Dennis McCoy, U.S.
1997	Street	Dave Mirra, U.S.	Dennis McCoy, U.S.	Dave Voelker, U.S.
1996	Street	Dave Mirra, U.S.	Jay Miron, Canada	Rob Nolli, U.S.
2005	Vert	Jamie Bestwick, Great Britain	Chad Kagy, U.S.	Kevin Robinson, U.S.
2004	Vert	Dave Mirra, U.S.	Simon Tabron, Great Britain	Kevin Robinson, U.S.
2003	Vert	Jamie Bestwick, Great Britain	Dave Mirra, U.S.	Kevin Robinson, U.S.
2002	Vert	Dave Mirra, U.S.	Mat Hoffman, U.S.	Simon Tabron, Great Britain
2001	Vert	Dave Mirra, U.S.	Jay Miron, Canada	Mat Hoffman, U.S.
2000	Vert	Jamie Bestwick, Great Britain	Dave Mirra, U.S.	Mat Hoffman, U.S.
1999	Vert	Dave Mirra, U.S.	Jay Miron, Canada	Simon Tabron, Great Britain
1998	Vert	Dave Mirra, U.S.	Dennis McCoy, U.S.	Simon Tabron, Great Britain
1997	Vert	Dave Mirra, U.S.	Dennis McCoy, U.S.	Mat Hoffman, U.S.
1996	Vert	Mat Hoffman, U.S.	Dave Mirra, U.S.	Jamie Bestwick, Great Britain
1995	Vert	Mat Hoffman, U.S.	Dave Mirra, U.S.	Jay Miron, Canada
2005	Vert Best Trick	Jamie Bestwick, Great Britain	Dave Mirra, U.S.	Chad Kagy, U.S.
1998	Vert Doubles	Dave Mirra, U.S. / Dennis McCoy, U.S.	Jay Miron, Canada / Dave Osato, Canada	Jason Davies, Great Britain / John Parker, U.S.

SUMMER GRAVITY GAMES RESULTS

YEAR	EVENT	GOLD	SILVER	BRONZE
2004	Street	Morgan Wade, U.S.	Ryan Nyquist, U.S.	Steven McCann, Australia
2003	Street	Dave Mirra, U.S.	Ryan Nyquist, U.S.	Steven McCann, Australia
2002	Street	Dave Mirra, U.S.	Ryan Nyquist, U.S.	Tom Haugen, U.S.
2001	Street	Ryan Nyquist, U.S.	Dave Osato, Canada	Chad Kagy, U.S.
2000	Street	Dave Osato, Canada	Ryan Nyquist, U.S.	Mike Laird, U.S.
1999	Street	Dave Mirra, U.S.	Ryan Nyquist, U.S.	Jay Miron, Canada
2005	Park	Gary Young, U.S.	Josh Harrington, U.S.	Alistair Whitton, Great Britain
2005	Dirt	Ryan Guettler, Australia	Luke Parslow, Australia	Joey Marks, U.S.
2004	Dirt	Ryan Nyquist, U.S.	Steven McCann, Australia	Stephen Murray, Great Britain
2003	Dirt	Ryan Nyquist, U.S.	Chris Doyle, U.S.	Steven McCann, Australia
2002	Dirt	Stephen Murray, Great Britain	Allan Cooke, U.S.	Chris Doyle, U.S.
2001	Dirt	Stephen Murray, Great Britain	Todd Walkowiak, U.S.	Chris Doyle, U.S.
2000	Dirt	T.J. Lavin, U.S.	Chris Doyle, U.S.	Ryan Jordan, U.S.
1999	Dirt	Ryan Nyquist, U.S.	Todd Walkowiak, U.S.	T.J. Lavin, U.S.
2005	Vert	Jamie Bestwick, Great Britain	Dennis McCoy, U.S.	Kevin Robinson, U.S.
2004	Vert	Jamie Bestwick, Great Britain	Chad Kagy, U.S.	Kevin Robinson, U.S.
2003	Vert	Dave Mirra, U.S.	Kevin Robinson, U.S.	Simon Tabron, Great Britain
2002	Vert	Simon Tabron, Great Britain	Dave Mirra, U.S.	Jay Miron, Canada
2001	Vert	Jamie Bestwick, Great Britain	Kevin Robinson, U.S.	Simon Tabron, Great Britain
2000	Vert	Dave Mirra, U.S.	Jamie Bestwick, Great Britain	Jay Miron, Canada
1999	Vert	Jamie Bestwick, Great Britain	Jay Miron, Canada	John Parker, U.S.
2005	Vert Best Trick	John Parker, U.S.	Chad Kagy, U.S.	Jamie Bestwick, Great Britain

DEW ACTION SPORTS TOUR RESULTS

YEAR	EVENT	GOLD	SILVER	BRONZE
2005	Dirt	Ryan Guettler, Australia	Corey Bohan, Australia	Cameron White, Australia
2005	Vert	Jamie Bestwick, Great Britain	Kevin Robinson, U.S.	Chad Kagy, U.S.
2005	Park	Ryan Guettler, Australia	Scotty Cranmer, U.S.	Ryan Nyquist, U.S.

LG ACTION SPORTS CHAMPIONSHIP RESULTS

YEAR	EVENT	GOLD	SILVER	BRONZE
2005	Street	Tobias Wicke, Germany	Dave Dillewaard, Australia	Diogo Canina, Brazil
2005	Vert	Jamie Bestwick, Great Britain	Chad Kagy, U.S.	Simon Tabron, Great Britain
2004	Vert	Jamie Bestwick, Great Britain	Simon Tabron, Great Britain	Kevin Robinson, U.S.
2004	Park	Ryan Nyquist, U.S.	Alistair Whitton, Great Britain	Scotty Cranmer, U.S.

1 CAMP WOODWARD, PENNSYLVANIA; LAKE OWEN, WISCONSIN; WOODWARD WEST, CALIFORNIA. The Woodward camps have it all: dirt jumps, halfpipes, street courses, and indoor and outdoor bowls. They also have training devices, such as foam pits and resi (soft) ramps, so riders can learn tough tricks safely.

Woodward West, California

2 AUSTIN, TEXAS. Many street spots in the state capital rule, but the best are found on the University of Texas campus. The rails, gaps, and ledges offer a real education in street riding.

3 VANCOUVER, BRITISH COLUMBIA, CANADA. The city has many great concrete parks, plus the Woodyard, an indoor facility with ramps for foul-weather riding. The parking lot next to the Indy Track downtown has smooth flat and banked sections for flatland tricks.

Vancouver, British Columbia, Canada

JEFF ZIELINSKI

4 NEW YORK CITY. The Big Apple has some of the most varied street terrain in the United States, including rails, ledges, benches, and curbs. Brooklyn Banks, part of a public park located underneath the Brooklyn Bridge, offers many banks, ledges, and walls.

5 SAN DIEGO, CALIFORNIA. The city has some famous skateparks, including the Magdalena Ecke Family YMCA in Encinitas. Other great terrain includes the mass of concrete drainage ditches around town.

New York City

6 GREENVILLE, NORTH CAROLINA. Pros such as Dave Mirra, Allan Cooke, Ryan Nyquist, and a dozen others call Greenville home. These pros can be found ripping ramps and other spots around town, especially in Jaycee Park, the scene of many photo shoots over the years.

Greenville, North Carolina

MARK LOSEY

7 QUEENSLAND, AUSTRALIA. The land down under has a ton of cement parks, especially in Queensland, near the state capital of Brisbane. This area has produced some of the talented Aussies now dominating BMX, including Ryan Guettler.

8 LOS ANGELES, CALIFORNIA. The best free spot in town is the "605 ditch." It is an area that runs for miles near Interstate 605 and includes banks, walls, ledges, and rails. One park worth visiting is called Alpine Skatepark in nearby Ventura, California. The park includes banks, bowls, ledges, and hips.

9 LONDON, ENGLAND. Europe has a slew of places to ride, but England probably offers the highest concentration of parks. There are a dozen in the London area alone, including some sweet spots that are free and open to the public.

Los Angeles, California

JEFF ZIELINSKI

10 NORTHEAST NEW JERSEY. This area outside New York City offers many awesome spots. The Centennial Avenue curb island in Piscataway is a tight manual pad in the middle of a parking lot. The pyramids at Montclair State University also provide a cool place to be seen riding.

Northeast New Jersey

JEFF ZIELINSKI

CHAPTER 2

IN-LINE SKATING

In-line skating was just a form of exercise
until the sport was taken into the air.

Eito Yasutoko won the
2005 World Vert title.

JESS DYRENFORTH

I n 1760, Joseph Merlin, a musical instrument and clock maker in London, England, attached metal wheels to his boots, creating the first in-line skates. He rode on them at a costume party and crashed into a wall-length mirror. Merlin's design, and all skates created for the next 100 years, featured wheels in-line (one wheel in front of another). However, these skates were difficult to control and stop.

In 1863, James Plimpton, a businessman from Medford, Massachusetts, invented a skate with pairs of wheels next to each other. These skates, known as quads, were easier to control than in-line models of the day and dominated skating for the next 100 years.

By the 1900's, roller rinks had opened all over the United States. Most people skated for recreation, but some competed in roller dancing and speed skating. During the 1970's, roller-skating and disco music blended into a fad known as roller disco, which renewed interest in roller-skating.

Takeshi Yasutoko (Eito's brother) won the 2004 World Vert title.

Year-round Training

By 1979, roller disco was fading in popularity. But Scott Olson, a hockey player in Minneapolis, Minnesota, discovered an old pair of in-line skates in a used sporting goods store. Olson recognized the similarities between in-line skates and ice skates. He set out to make a pair that would allow him to practice his hockey skills year-round. Olson and his brother Brennan used hockey skate boots to make an in-line skate in his parents' basement. New technology, including the urethane wheel, made the Olsons' in-line model safer and easier to maneuver than those of the past.

The Birth of Rollerblade

In 1980, the Olsons founded an in-line skate company. Three years later, the company became Rollerblade, Inc. It launched a revolution in roller sports. The Olsons sold Rollerblade to a group of investors in 1984. At the time, most in-line skaters were cross-country skiers and hockey players who used their skates for cross-training.

In 1988, Rollerblade unveiled the Lightning TRS model. The TRS had a molded plastic boot and improved wheel and bearing protection, making in-line skates safer and more reliable. With improved design and easy-to-use rear brakes, Rollerblades were now amateur-friendly.

Around the same time, Rollerblade formed a team of riders to promote its skates. The team performed skateboard-inspired stunts on quarterpipes at sporting events and trade shows around the world. By 1990, some members of the team, including Chris Edwards, were pioneering a style of skating called aggressive in-line.

Time to Soar

Aggressive in-line skaters adapted skateboard tricks, such as aerials and grinds, to streets and ramps. In 1993, a series of innovations transformed aggressive in-line into a full-fledged sport. That year, Edwards was featured in the first in-line video, *Dare to Air.* In one segment, he jumped onto a handrail while skating. The move made skaters realize more daring tricks were possible.

Also in 1993, pro skater Arlo Eisenberg helped launch Senate, the first company that made hardware for aggressive in-line. Two hardware innovations — grind plates and smaller wheels — made riding handrails easier. And two magazines, *Box* and *Daily Bread,* dedicated to the new in-line scene, published their first issues.

Height of Popularity

In 1994, the National In-line Skate Series and Aggressive Skaters Association, both nationwide sanctioning bodies, were formed and began holding contests. Skating's popularity was at an all-time high.

In 1995, aggressive in-line got its first true skate, the Roces Majestic 12. The Majestic 12 had a space on the frame for grinding. (Previously, skaters modified their own skates with skateboard wheels and homemade grind plates.) Also in 1995, the Extreme Games, now known as the X Games, made its debut. It featured the following in-line disciplines: Men's Downhill, Vert, and Street, and Women's Vert.

Meanwhile, skaters such as Randy Spizer and Jon Julio continued to push the progression of street riding. Spizer brought a smooth style to moves, such as backslides performed on new terrain like ledges and planters. Julio demonstrated a new realm of tricks, including fishbrains and topside acids (types of grinds).

By the late 1990's, the popularity of aggressive in-line skating began to decline in the United States. Young athletes were choosing to skateboard instead of in-line skate. Aggressive in-line was eliminated from some action sports events as well. In 2005, it was dropped from the X Games.

Rising Hope

A new generation of skaters has emerged to push trick progression in vert and street. The Yasutoko brothers, Eito and Takeshi, rule the ramp. These Japanese brothers go huge with style. Chris Haffey of San Diego, California, blows minds with the innovative street tricks he performs in videos.

Even though the sport is no longer a part of the X Games, competitive aggressive in-line continues to roll. Skaters compete on the ASA Pro Tour, for the LG Action Sports Championship, and in other major contests worldwide. The future of the sport is shaky, but skaters are trying new tricks and still having fun.

INNOVATOR

FABIOLA DA SILVA

Fabiola da Silva began skating in 1995 in her hometown of São Paulo, Brazil. Her skills developed quickly. In 1996, she won the X Games Vert contest. With a combination of raw talent and style, she would win the event three years in a row. In all, da Silva has won more medals than any other woman at the X Games, including a total of seven gold medals in Vert and Park. By 2002, it was clear other women could not compete with da Silva, so she began to compete against men. In 2004, da Silva ranked fifth in Vert on the ASA men's pro tour. In June 2005, she became the first woman to land a double backflip on a vert ramp. By adding the move to her routine, she finished fourth in Vert at the 2005 World Championships.

JESS DYRENFORTH

‹ U P – A N D – C O M E R ›
DAVID SIZEMORE

Few people in aggressive in-line skating circles had heard of David Sizemore before the summer of 2005. But all that changed at the ASA Americas Amateur Championships in Sacramento, California. He beat the competition by a huge margin. The 15-year-old from Alpharetta, Georgia, put together a street run that would have been good enough to beat some of the best pros. He opened his run with a gap disaster frontside royale (a jump landing in a grind move), followed with flawless technical tricks, and finished with a 540 to alley oop soul (a 1 ½-spin landing in a backward grind). Now that he's made his mark, expect more super-sized tricks from Sizemore.

ISAAC AIKEN

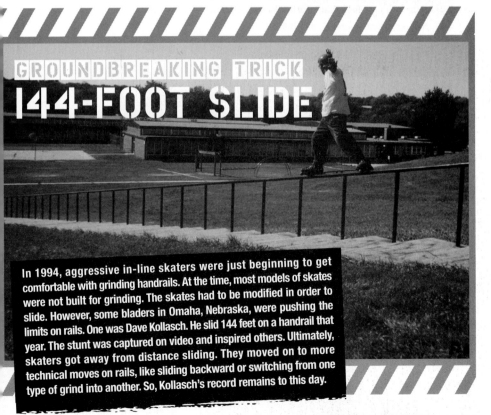

GROUNDBREAKING TRICK
144-FOOT SLIDE

In 1994, aggressive in-line skaters were just beginning to get comfortable with grinding handrails. At the time, most models of skates were not built for grinding. The skates had to be modified in order to slide. However, some bladers in Omaha, Nebraska, were pushing the limits on rails. One was Dave Kollasch. He slid 144 feet on a handrail that year. The stunt was captured on video and inspired others. Ultimately, skaters got away from distance sliding. They moved on to more technical moves on rails, like sliding backward or switching from one type of grind into another. So, Kollasch's record remains to this day.

THE BASIC TRICKS

FRONTSIDE GRIND ▶

The frontside requires the skater to jump onto the rail or ledge and turn 90 degrees so that the skates are perpendicular to the edge. Both front and rear skates grind on the inside of the grind plate.

ALEX SCHELBERT/DE/RED BULL

STEVE BOYLE/NEWSPORT

180 SPIN ▲

A 180 spin is a basic half-spin. It can be practiced first on flat ground by jumping and turning halfway around, and then landing backward. Once comfortable, the skater can progress to curbs and ledges before trying the spin on ramps and adding different grabs.

MUTE GRAB ▶

A mute grab first requires getting air. Once airborne, the rider reaches across the front of his body and grabs his skate. If he uses his right hand, he grabs his left skate. If he uses his left hand, he grabs his right skate.

SJAAK VAN DER LINDEN/RED BULL

TIME LINE

1760 Joseph Merlin creates the first in-line skates in England.

1863 James Plimpton of Medford, Massachusetts, invents the quad skate, an improvement over the in-line skates of the day.

1980 Using an ice hockey boot, Scott Olson creates an in-line skate. He starts a company to manufacture them.

1983 Olson's company becomes Rollerblade, Inc. He sell it to a group of investor the following year.

<GREATEST MOMENT>
CHRIS EDWARDS'S SLIDE ON A HANDRAIL

Chris Edwards got his start on wheels as a quad roller skater growing up in Southern California. By the late 1980's, he had switched to in-line skates and become a member of Rollerblade's demonstration team. He soon earned a reputation as a wild man who would try any trick. He really became famous in 1993 with his part in the first aggressive in-line video, *Dare to Air.* While filming in Atlanta, Georgia, Edwards jumped onto a handrail with his skates and slid down the rail. The footage stunned viewers and expanded notions of what was possible on skates. Edwards continued to innovate, eventually winning bronze medals in both Vert and Street at the 1996 and 1997 X Games. Today, he is a featured character in Acclaim Entertainment's *Aggressive Inline* video game.

Edwards, here in 2004, is still wowing crowds with his daring moves.

JESS DYRENFORTH

FAST FACT
Many people refer to in-line skating as Rollerblading. They are wrong. In-line skating is a sport; Rollerblade is a company that makes skates.

1987 Team Rollerblade begins demonstrating skates and ramp riding to promote the company's skates.

1988 Rollerblade introduces the Lightning TRS, the first successful mass-marketed in-line skate.

1992 Homemade grind plates and anti-rocker wheels are developed to expand the possibilities of grind tricks.

1993 Two aggressive in-line skating magazines, *Box* and *Daily Bread,* begin publishing.

COURTESY OF DAILY BREAD

< LEGEND >
CESAR MORA

Cesar Mora played soccer while growing up in Australia. He was good enough to be offered a contract by a pro team in Spain. But Mora didn't want to leave his home and turned down the offer. In 1994, Mora began in-line skating around the city of Sydney. He found he loved blading as much as soccer and began trying out tricks on the streets and ramps. His reputation grew among fellow skaters. By 1995, Mora was invited to compete in the first X Games. He won a silver medal in Vert by getting huge air and performing flat spins and combos. He went on to win the pro tour that year. He has competed in every X Games Vert final. He won gold at the Games in 1998, silver in 1999, and bronze in 2000. Mora's explosive approach to ramp riding still sets the standard for the sport.

F⒜⒮⒯ FACT
Pro Matt Lindenmuth is a double sports threat. In addition to competing in in-line, he is a pro snowboarder. He finished 18th in Superpipe at the 2004 Winter Gravity Games.

TIME LINE

1994 The National In-line Skate Series and the Aggressive Skaters Association, the sport's first sanctioning bodies, form and begin holding contests.

1995 The Extreme Games debut in Providence, Rhode Island, and include Men's Downhill, Vert, and Street, and Women's Vert.

CHRIS MITCHELL

The first X Games

1997 The first annual Showdown at the Hoedown contest is held at Eisenbergs Skatepark, in Plano, Texas.

1998 The Univers Frame System is developed. It allows skate parts, such as wheels, to be used c various skates.

NECESSARY OBJECTS

- **SKATES:** There are three types of skate boots: hard boot, soft boot, and hybrid. The hard boot contains a removable liner surrounded by a hard plastic shell. The soft boot doesn't have a hard protective covering and offers a greater range of motion than a hard boot. The hybrid is made of plastic, but offers a greater range of motion than a hard boot. The latest design innovation comes from Xsjado (pronounced "shadow"), which has a shoe instead of a liner. The removable shoe straps into the boot.

  All boots sit on a chassis. The chassis holds the wheels on the boot. It can be made from aluminum, carbon, magnesium, or even plastic. Street skates often have an H-Block between the second and third wheels. The H-Block is a flat plate used for grinding. Some street chassis have only two wheels (most skates have four), offering more area to grind on.

  Wheels vary according to size and hardness. A wheel's hardness level is called its durometer. A higher durometer, or harder wheel, is best for street or rough surfaces, and tends to be faster. Lower durometer wheels work better indoors and offer better grip.

  Wheels also come in different setups. The most common is four on each skate in a flat rocker position. This is where all four wheels are the same size and touch the ground when the skate is flat. Flat rocker is great for skating, but doesn't work well for grinding. Those who ride street and want to grind often can create an anti-rocker setup. Anti-rocker uses smaller and harder wheels in the second and third positions. However, such a setup makes the skate slower.

  Bearings are placed inside the wheels to let them roll easily. All bearings are rated according to ABEC (Annular Bearing Engineers' Committee) standards. The best-performing bearings have a higher number on the ABEC scale. ABEC 9 is best, followed by 7, then 5, 3, and finally 1. However, a novice won't notice much difference in performance between a 1 and 3.

- **HELMET:** After skates, a helmet is the most important piece of equipment. The helmet should be CSPC (U.S. Consumer Product Safety Commission) rated. Today, pro street bladers are often shown in magazines and videos without helmets. But vert skaters almost always wear them.

- **PADS:** The best knee and elbow pads come with plastic caps, which absorb a blow and will slide on rough surfaces. Wrist guards are especially good for beginners, who often try to break a fall with their hands. Pads should fit properly and not slip down during a slam.

000 The IMYTA (atch Your Trick ociation) is created. It ds underground tests with only a few ct skaters.

2001 Matt Lindenmuth lands one of the first double backflips.

Matt Lindenmuth

CHRIS MITCHELL

2003 The annual LG Action Sports Championship is launched, crowning a champ in Men's and Women's Street and Vert.

2005 The X Games drops all aggressive in-line events. At the World Championships, Eito Yasutoko wins Vert and Chris Haffey wins Street.

TOP 10 ATHLETES

1 EITO YASUTOKO, born July 29, 1983, in Osaka, Japan. Eito is the most dominant vert rider ever. He and his younger brother, Takeshi, grew up riding a halfpipe at their father's roller rink in Osaka, Japan. Eito won his first X Games gold medal in 1999 at age 16. He has since won two more gold medals, in 2000 and 2003, and bronze in 2004. Eito is tough to beat because of his combination of technical skill and flair. In 2005, he won his second World Vert title.

2 TAKESHI YASUTOKO, born June 25, 1986, in Osaka, Japan. Brother Eito is the only person standing in the way of Takeshi's dominance. In 2004, not even Eito could stop Takeshi, who was world champion, Number 1 on the pro tour, and X Games Vert gold medalist. Takeshi began competing on the pro tour at age 9 and first competed in the X Games at 11. He also won X Games gold in 2002.

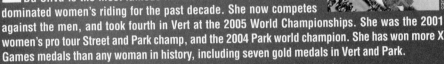

Takeshi Yasutoko

SIMON YAP/ESPN IMAGES

3 FABIOLA DA SILVA, born June 18, 1979, in São Paulo, Brazil. Da Silva is the most famous in-line skater in the world. She dominated women's riding for the past decade. She now competes against the men, and took fourth in Vert at the 2005 World Championships. She was the 2001 women's pro tour Street and Park champ, and the 2004 Park world champion. She has won more X Games medals than any woman in history, including seven gold medals in Vert and Park.

4 CHRIS HAFFEY, born January 7, 1985, in San Diego, California. Haffey is famous for bringing real street style into park contests. He has raised the level of skating with his big gaps and rail tricks. He won the world championship in Street in 2004 and 2005.

5 JEFF STOCKWELL, born June 18, 1984, in San Clemente, California. This 21-year-old is a video star who competes as well. He finished fourth at the 2005 World Championships.

JESS DYRENFORTH

Marc Englehart

6 MARC ENGLEHART, born February 27, 1983, in Sellersville, Pennsylvania. Englehart is a master of the 1080. In 2002, he won Vert at the Gravity Games, placed third at the X Games, and ranked second on the pro tour. In 2003, he finished third at the Gravity Games.

7 BRIAN SHIMA, born December 22, 1981, in Redwood City, California. This street legend is a smooth, aggressive skater. He won a bronze medal at the 2005 World Championships.

8 BRUNO LOWE, born July 18, 1981, in Munich, Germany. Lowe is a street skater who goes high. He is a legend in Europe, where most fans know him through his roles in videos. Lowe won X Games gold in Street in 2003 and silver in 2002.

9 RICHIE VELASQUEZ, born January 14, 1976, in Brooklyn, New York. Velasquez did not turn pro until 2002, when he was 26. He is a fan favorite at contests because of his fearless attack. Velasquez won the 2003 Gravity Games gold medal in Street Best Trick.

10 FALLON HEFFERNAN, born August 29, 1986, in Jacksonville, Florida. The 2005 world champion in Street has been a pro since age 13. She placed third in 2004 at the World Championships and has won X Games silver in 2001 and bronze in 2002.

X GAMES RESULTS

MEN

YEAR	EVENT	GOLD	SILVER	BRONZE
2003	Park	Bruno Lowe, Germany	Stephane Alfano, France	Sven Boekhorst, Netherlands
2002	Park	Jaren Grob, U.S.	Bruno Lowe, Germany	Blake Dennis, Australia
2001	Park	Jaren Grob, U.S.	Louie Zamora, U.S.	Franky Morales, U.S.
2000	Park	Sven Boekhorst, Netherlands	Jaren Grob, U.S.	Sam Fogarty, Australia
1999	Street	Nicky Adams, Canada	Blake Dennis, Australia	Aaron Feinberg, U.S.
1998	Street	Jonathan Bergeron, Canada	Marco Hintze, Mexico	Aaron Feinberg, U.S.
1997	Street	Aaron Feinberg, U.S.	Tim Ward, Australia	Chris Edwards, U.S.
1996	Street	Arlo Eisenberg, U.S.	Matt Mantz, U.S.	Chris Edwards, U.S.
1995	Street	Matt Salerno, Australia	Scott Bentley, New Zealand	Ryan Jacklone, U.S.
2004	Vert	Takeshi Yasutoko, Japan	Marco de Santi, Brazil	Eito Yasutoko, Japan
2003	Vert	Eito Yasutoko, Japan	Takeshi Yasutoko, Japan	Nel Martin, Spain
2002	Vert	Takeshi Yasutoko, Japan	Eito Yasutoko, Japan	Marc Englehart, U.S.
2001	Vert	Taig Khris, France	Takeshi Yasutoko, Japan	Shane Yost, Tasmania
2000	Vert	Eito Yasutoko, Japan	Takeshi Yasutoko, Japan	Cesar Mora, Australia
1999	Vert	Eito Yasutoko, Japan	Cesar Mora, Australia	Matt Salerno, Australia
1998	Vert	Cesar Mora, Australia	Matt Salerno, Australia	Taig Khris, France
1997	Vert	Tim Ward, Australia	Taig Khris, France	Chris Edwards, U.S.
1996	Vert	Rene Hulgreen, Denmark	Tom Fry, Australia	Chris Edwards, U.S.
1995	Vert	Tom Fry, Australia	Cesar Mora, Australia	Manuel Billiris, Australia
1999	Vert Triples	Sven Boekhorst, Netherlands	Mike Budnik, U.S.	Maki Komori, Japan
		Javier Bujanda, Spain	Cesar Mora, Australia	Eito Yasutoko, Japan
		Taig Khris, France	Matt Salerno, Australia	Takeshi Yasutoko, Japan
1998	Vert Triples	Paul Malina, Australia	Mike Budnik, U.S.	Sven Boekhorst, Netherlands
		Viorel Popa, U.S.	Cesar Mora, Australia	Javier Bujanda, Spain
		Sam Fogarty, Australia	Matt Salerno, Australia	Taig Khris, France
1996	Best Trick	Dion Antony, Australia	Ryan Jacklone, U.S.	Eric Schrijn, U.S.
1995	Best Trick	B. Hardin, U.S.	Ryan Jacklone, U.S.	Brooke Howard-Smith, New Zealand
1995	High Air	Chris Edwards, U.S.	Manuel Billiris, Australia	Ichi Komori, Japan

WOMEN

YEAR	EVENT	GOLD	SILVER	BRONZE
2003	Park	Fabiola da Silva, Brazil	Jenny Logue, Great Britain	Martina Svobodova, Slovakia
2002	Park	Martina Svobodova, Slovakia	Jenna Downing, Great Britain	Fallon Heffernan, U.S.
2001	Park	Martina Svobodova, Slovakia	Fallon Heffernan, U.S.	Anneke Winter, Germany
2000	Park	Fabiola da Silva, Brazil	Martina Svobodova, Slovakia	Kelly Matthews, U.S.
1999	Street	Sayaka Yabe, Japan	Kelly Matthews, U.S.	Jenny Curry, U.S.
1998	Street	Jenny Curry, U.S.	Salima Sanga, Switzerland	Sayaka Yabe, Japan
1997	Street	Sayaka Yabe, Japan	Katie Brown, U.S.	True Otis, U.S.
2001	Vert	Fabiola da Silva, Brazil	Ayumi Kawasaki, Japan	Not awarded
2000	Vert	Fabiola da Silva, Brazil	Ayumi Kawasaki, Japan	Merce Borrull, Spain
1999	Vert	Ayumi Kawasaki, Japan	Fabiola da Silva, Brazil	Maki Komori, Japan
1998	Vert	Fabiola da Silva, Brazil	Ayumi Kawasaki, Japan	Maki Komori, Japan
1997	Vert	Fabiola da Silva, Brazil	Claudia Trachsel, Switzerland	Ayumi Kawasaki, Japan
1996	Vert	Fabiola da Silva, Brazil	Jodie Tyler, Australia	Tasha Hodgson, Australia
1995	Vert	Tasha Hodgson, Australia	Angie Walton, New Zealand	Laura Connery, U.S.

GRAVITY GAMES RESULTS

MEN

YEAR	EVENT	GOLD	SILVER	BRONZE
2003	Street Best Trick	Richie Velasquez, U.S.	Stephane Alfano, France	Brian Aragon, U.S.
2002	Street Best Trick	Aaron Feinberg, U.S.	Brian Shima, U.S.	Jaren Grob, U.S.
2001	Street	Blake Dennis, Australia	Louie Zamora, U.S.	Aaron Feinberg, U.S.
2000	Street	Sven Boekhorst, Netherlands	Blake Dennis, Australia	Wilfried Rossignol, France
1999	Street	Sven Boekhorst, Netherlands	Louie Zamora, U.S.	Mike Budnik, U.S.
2003	Vert	Eito Yasutoko, Japan	Marco de Santi, Brazil	Marc Englehart, U.S.
2002	Vert	Marc Englehart, U.S.	Takeshi Yasutoko, Japan	Shane Yost, Tasmania
2001	Vert	Taig Khris, France	Takeshi Yasutoko, Japan	Matt Lindenmuth, U.S.
2000	Vert	Matt Salerno, Australia	Taig Khris, France	Eito Yasutoko, Japan
1999	Vert	Taig Khris, France	Shane Yost, Tasmania	Cesar Mora, Australia

WOMEN

YEAR	EVENT	GOLD	SILVER	BRONZE
2000	Street	Martina Svobodova, Slovakia	Fabiola da Silva, Brazil	Kelly Matthews, U.S.
1999	Street	Fabiola da Silva, Brazil	Anneke Winter, Germany	Kelly Matthews, U.S.
2001	Vert	Ayumi Kawasaki, Japan	Fabiola da Silva, Brazil	Not awarded
2000	Vert	Fabiola da Silva, Brazil	Ayumi Kawasaki, Japan	Merce Borrull, Spain
1999	Vert	Fabiola da Silva, Brazil	Merce Borrull, Spain	Maki Komori, Japan

LG ACTION SPORTS CHAMPIONSHIP

MEN

YEAR	EVENT	GOLD	SILVER	BRONZE
2005	Street	Chris Haffey, U.S.	Carl Hills, U.S.	Brian Shima, U.S.
2004	Street	Chris Haffey, U.S.	Erik Bailey, U.S.	Richie Velasquez, U.S.
2003	Street	Blake Dennis, Australia	Brian Aragon, U.S.	Jeff Stockwell, U.S.
2002	Street	Blake Dennis, Australia	Ryan Dawes, U.S.	Stephane Alfano, France
2001	Street	Jaren Grob, U.S.	Aaron Feinberg, U.S.	Thierry Lallemand, France
2000	Street	Sven Boekhorst, Netherlands	Blake Dennis, Australia	Thierry Lallemand, France
2005	Vert	Eito Yasutoko, Japan	Takeshi Yasutoko, Japan	Shane Yost, Tasmania
2004	Vert	Takeshi Yasutoko, Japan	Marco de Santi, Brazil	Shane Yost, Tasmania
2003	Vert	Eito Yasutoko, Japan	Shane Yost, Tasmania	Marco de Santi, Brazil
2002	Vert	Takeshi Yasutoko, Japan	Shane Yost, Tasmania	Marc Englehart, U.S.
2001	Vert	Taig Khris, France	Takeshi Yasutoko, Japan	Eito Yasutoko, Japan
2000	Vert	Taig Khris, France	Tobias Bucher, Germany	Takeshi Yasutoko, Japan

WOMEN

YEAR	EVENT	GOLD	SILVER	BRONZE
2005	Street	Fallon Heffernan, U.S.	Katie Ketchum, U.S.	Jenna Downing, England
2004	Street	Fabiola da Silva, Brazil	Katie Ketchum, U.S.	Fallon Heffernan, U.S.
2003	Street	Martina Svobodova, Slovakia	Fabiola da Silva, Brazil	Fallon Heffernan, U.S.
2002	Street	Martina Svobodova, Slovakia	Fallon Heffernan, U.S.	Deborah West, U.S.
2001	Street	Martina Svobodova, Slovakia	Fabiola da Silva, Brazil	Anneke Winter, Germany
2000	Street	Martina Svobodova, Slovakia	Fabiola da Silva, Brazil	Fallon Heffernan, U.S.
2001	Vert	Fabiola da Silva, Brazil	Ayumi Kawasaki, Japan	Katie Brown, U.S.
2000	Vert	Fabiola da Silva, Brazil	Ayumi Kawasaki, Japan	Katie Brown, U.S.

TOP 10 PLACES TO RIDE

1 WOODWARD CAMPS: CAMP WOODWARD, PENNSYLVANIA; WOODWARD WEST, CALIFORNIA; LAKE OWEN, WISCONSIN. These three are the ultimate in terrain and training facilities. They are a skater's paradise and contain dozens of indoor and outdoor street courses, vert ramps, and bowls. Sleepover camps are held during the summer, but top pros live there year-round. Athletes train using the foam pits and resi ramps. The facilities allow skaters to learn tricks without risking serious injury.

JESS DYRENFORTH

2 EISENBERGS SKATEPARK, PLANO, TEXAS. The park is owned by the family of pro skater Arlo Eisenberg. It offers 30,000 square feet of rails, ramps, ledges, and stairs. There are two indoor courses: one for beginners and another for advanced bladers.

Woodward West, California

3 GOODSKATES, OSAKA, JAPAN. This is an outdoor skatepark owned by Takeshi and Eito Yasutoko's father, Yuki. Goodskates consists of a halfpipe, mini-half, street course, and a bowl.

4 LOS ANGELES, CALIFORNIA, STREETS. Many schools in the L.A. area have rails, banks, and ledges. Downtown L.A. has great urban terrain on every block. Glendale Verdugo Skatepark, a concrete park, features bowls, ledges, hips, and banks.

CHRIS MITCHELL

5 SAN DIEGO, CALIFORNIA, STREETS. San Diego boasts great weather and skating spots all around the city. For an advanced degree in grinding, riders can go to some of the area's universities, such as San Diego State and the University of San Diego. Both offer rails and ledges galore.

Barcelona, Spain

6 BARCELONA, SPAIN, STREETS. The public squares and marble steps of the city's many churches are fair game for skaters. The best spots are the ledges and benches at the Museum of Contemporary Art and at the Port Olympic Skatepark.

7 MAGDALENA ECKE FAMILY YMCA SKATEPARK, ENCINITAS, CALIFORNIA. This park has everything, including a challenging street section, concrete pools, and the 13-foot-tall, 160-foot-long halfpipe from the Global X Games.

8 BONDI BEACH, SYDNEY, AUSTRALIA. Bowl-A-Rama, a massive new public concrete skatepark with bowls and hips, opened in 2005. It's right on the sand at Bondi Beach. Bondi is a longtime haunt of bladers, including pro Cesar Mora, who got his start on a ramp in the area.

9 PARIS, FRANCE. Skaters say *"merci"* for the city's miles of street terrain. Rollerparc Avenue has one of the largest skateparks. It features two bowls, four street courses, three mini-ramps, a speed track, and a halfpipe.

10 BROOKLYN BANKS, NEW YORK CITY. The banks are located at the base of the Brooklyn Bridge on the Manhattan side. They offer a series of brick-paved banks, with ledges, rails, and walls. It is part of a public park and can be skated with no hassles.

CHAPTER 3

MOTOCROSS

The man who invented the motorcycle never dreamed what action sports athletes would do with his machine.

Travis Pastrana has won five freestyle gold medals at the X Games.

M. PAULSEN/SHAZAMM/ESPN

Gottlieb Daimler created the first gasoline-powered motorcycle in 1885. Daimler, a German engineer, attached a new type of engine to a wooden bicycle. The engine was called a four-stroke engine because it was powered by four movements, or strokes, of its pistons per cycle: intake, compression, power, and exhaust. This is the same type of engine used in cars today.

Daimler went on to use his engine design to make one of the first automobiles, but other engineers and sportsmen continued to experiment with motorcycles. The earliest motorcycles that came after Daimler's were also made from bicycles. In those days, motorcycles were hugely popular because they were more affordable than cars.

Bubba Stewart won 11 national racing titles as an amateur.

BO BRIDGES

Racing Is Born

By the 1900's, manufacturers were organizing races to show off their products. Hill climbs, races on horse- and bike-tracks, and days-long endurance trials were the most popular motorcyle events.

In 1924, a motorcycle club in England hosted a cross-country race over a long, 2.5-mile course. They called it a "scramble" because racers scrambled over steep hills and other types of rough terrain. Scrambling became a big sport in England and eventually made its way to the rest of Europe.

In France, race organizers added man-made jumps and changed the race to several times around a smaller course, which made it more popular with spectators. They called the new style of racing "motocross," a combination of "motorcycle" and "cross-country." By 1957, motocross had become so popular in Europe that a world-championship race was created.

Giants Steps in Design

Early motocross bikes were primitive by today's standards. They were heavy, underpowered, and not built to handle rough terrain. New developments in design made them more durable, and by 1958 smaller and lighter 250cc two-stroke engines began to replace the bigger, older four-stroke models in motorcycle racing.

The term *cc* stands for cubic centimeters, which measures the size of an engine's chambers. The larger the chamber, the more powerful the engine. However, the introduction of the two-stroke engine changed the equation. A two-stroke engine requires two strokes of the piston per cycle instead of four. Therefore, a two-stroke engine fires twice as often, which makes it more powerful than a four-stroke engine of the same size. (Two-stroke engines also pollute more and use fuel less efficiently. They are used mostly in chain saws, Jet Skis, outboard motors, and, of course, motorcycles.)

This move to smaller and more powerful engines was soon joined by the use of smaller and lighter materials in motorcycle frames. Husqvarna, a Swedish company, introduced these new frames, which allowed riders to soar higher over jumps and race faster. These bikes began to arrive in the United States during the 1960's, but

Kevin Windham
has been runner-up for
the motocross title
four times.

many Americans weren't impressed. In 1966, a clever salesman named Edison Dye brought over the top European riders to demonstrate what the lightweight bikes could do. Most Americans had seen only scrambles and not true motocross racing. They were thrilled by the speed and acrobatic moves of the Europeans.

Motocross began to grow in the United States. In 1967, a national tour revved up, featuring Europeans and Americans. Riders competed for the championship by accumulating points in a series of races. In 1969, *ABC's Wide World of Sports* became the first television show to broadcast a motorcycle race: a motocross event in Massachusetts. At this time, the American Motorcyclist Association (AMA) began holding races regularly.

By 1972, the AMA had organized the National Championship Motocross Series, which absorbed the earlier tour. European riders, especially Roger DeCoster, continued to dominate competition. DeCoster won four straight AMA championships from 1974 to 1977.

Here Comes Supercross

Soon after the arrival of motocross in the United States,

race promoters began trying out a new type of track that could be built in arenas. In 1971, the AMA held the first pro race on a temporary track at Daytona International Speedway. Stadium races followed at the Houston Astrodome and Los Angeles Coliseum. Eventually the term *supercross* was used to describe the new events, combining "Super Bowl" and "motocross." Supercross became popular because the races were shorter, and it was easier for fans to watch from the stands than from alongside a mile-long motocross track.

DeCoster was still the dominant rider in both motocross and supercross, but by the late 1970's American stars began to emerge. The first was Bob "Hurricane" Hannah, who won the AMA

FAST FACT

The abbreviation *cc* stands for cubic centimeters and refers to an engine's power. For example, a 125cc motorcycle is more powerful than an 80cc engine, but less powerful than a 250cc.

supercross championship from 1977 through 1979.

American riders, led by Rick Johnson who won a combined five titles in supercross and motocross, took over the sport during the 1980's. Jeff Stanton, another American, won a total of six supercross and motocross titles from 1989 through 1992.

Because the sport was still new, there were not a lot of rules. Some of the early champs won races on suped-up bikes made with lighter parts and more powerful engines than their opponents. But by 1986, the AMA changed the rules, requiring racing bikes to meet the same standards as those sold to the public. This made competition more even and boosted motorcycle sales; people wanted to ride the same bikes as the sport's stars. By this time, the biggest motorcycle manufacturers were in Japan: companies such as Honda, Yamaha, Kawasaki, and Suzuki. They continue to dominate the market today.

Freestyle Arrives

By the 1990's supercross was king, and Jeremy McGrath wore its crown. The former BMX racer from California won a record seven titles from 1993 through 2000. In 1997, the only year he didn't win, McGrath finished second, after missing races due to injuries. He also won the motocross championship in 1995.

Meanwhile, BMX, which had been inspired by motocross during the 1960's, began to inspire motocross. Freestyle BMX riders had invented hundreds of tricks, and motocross racers began trying them out while soaring 50 feet over jumps. For example, McGrath would pull nacnacs — kicking one foot over the back of his bike to the other side — while launching during races. Fans loved it. Another Californian, Mike Metzger, became known as the "godfather" of freestyle for helping to develop the discipline during the mid-1990's.

Freestyle began having its own judged competitions, first as sideshows during motocross and supercross

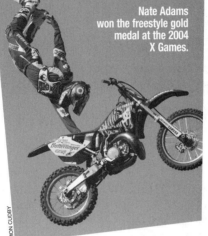

Nate Adams won the freestyle gold medal at the 2004 X Games.

SIMON CUDBY

races. By the late 1990's, freestyle riders began to organize their own shows. One of the first was the Crusty Demons Tour, begun in 1996.

Freestyle got a huge boost in 1999, when the event was added to the X Games lineup. During its debut, a 15-year-old hotshot named Travis Pastrana wowed the crowd, won the gold medal, and launched himself and his motorcycle into San Francisco Bay as an encore. Ever since, freestyle motocross, now known as FMX, has been one of the X Games' most popular sports.

Pastrana has continued to dominate FMX. He has won gold medals in five of his six tries at the X Games. Meanwhile, the difficulty of tricks has progressed to mind-boggling levels. In 2002, Metzger nailed back-to-back backflips. Now all the top riders can pull backflips, and some can even do 360 backflips. In 2004, Chuck Carothers pulled his signature Carolla at the X Games, by letting go of his bike and spinning his body sideways before grabbing on again.

The Race Is On

Back on the racetrack, Ricky Carmichael has taken McGrath's accomplishments and done him one better. The 26-year-old is rewriting the record books. He has won the 250cc motocross title every year since 2000 (six straight times). He's the only rider to finish a season undefeated, doing it three times (2002, 2004, and 2005). Add in his four supercross titles (2001-2003, and 2005), and you have the most dominant motorcycle rider ever. He's already the all-time winningest rider in motocross history, and could close in on McGrath's supercross record of 72 career wins in a few years.

It's hard to imagine anyone ever topping Carmichael, but young stars, such as James Stewart, Chad Reed, and Ernesto Fonseca have tons of talent and desire. Plus, young FMX riders such as Nate Adams and Jeremy Stenberg keep pushing the progression of newer and more exciting tricks. Whether it's supercross, FMX, or motocross, the riders keep getting better every year.

INNOVATOR

CAREY HART

He has his own reality show on TV, *Inked,* about his tattoo studio in Las Vegas, Nevada. He's married to singer Pink. But before he became a television celebrity, Carey Hart was a freestyle motocross pioneer famous for pulling the sport's first backflip on a 250cc motorcycle. Before Hart, only Jose Yanez and Bob Kohl, two former pro BMX riders, had done backflips. But they had done their flips on small motorcycles. No one wanted to risk serious injury by attempting one on a 250cc bike. Then, at the 2000 Gravity Games, both Hart and Travis Pastrana went for the backflip. They had been practicing on specially-designed courses at the Woodward Camp in Pennsylvania. Hart was the only one to land it, but he slid out while riding away. Hart tried a backflip again at the 2001 X Games, but he fell 40 feet and broke 14 bones in his foot, several ribs, and bruised his tailbone. In spite of that, other freestyle riders began practicing the backflip. By 2002 several riders had done the move in practice, and Caleb Wyatt had done backflips that were captured on video. At the X Games that year, Hart, Pastrana, Mike Metzger, and Kenny Bartram all flipped out. Today, all the top riders can backflip because Carey Hart had the courage to show it was possible.

BO BRIDGES

‹GREATEST MOMENT›
TRAVIS PASTRANA'S SLAM DUNK

Travis Pastrana knows how to make a splash at a freestyle motocross contest. In 1999, when Pastrana was only 15, freestyle motocross made its debut at the X Games in San Francisco, California. Already a showman, Pastrana raced around the course, pulling a no-handed heelclicker and a one-handed Superman. With a near-flawless first run in the finals, Pastrana received a score of 99.0. With one run remaining, he decided to go for a crazy stunt. He launched off one of the jumps, sailed 100 feet off the course on his motorcycle, and landed with a splash in San Francisco Bay. The stunt cost him $10,000 in fines, but paid off in other ways. He became the world's most famous freestyler. Since then, he has backed up his brash act with four more gold medals in Freestyle.

Only 5' 7" tall, James "Bubba" Stewart has big plans – to dominate motocross and supercross for a long time. Ever since Stewart was a kid smoking all comers in the amateur ranks, fans have been waiting to see him race the world's best. He won more races than any rider in amateur history, collecting 11 national titles. In 2002 he turned pro at age 17 and dominated the 125cc series by winning the Motocross title and finishing second in Supercross. He was AMA Motocross/Supercross Rookie of the Year. Stewart won back-to-back motocross and supercross titles over the next two seasons. He finally moved up to the 250cc class full-time in 2005, and won three races in the supercross series. However, he finished 10th overall after missing 10 races because of an injury. Still just 20, the little guy needs only a combination of experience and good health to produce big things in years to come.

PHIL ELLSWORTH

GROUNDBREAKING TRICK
BACKFLIP

MIKE METZGER

For years, freestyle motocross riders dreamed of pulling a backflip during competition but were afraid to try. Carey Hart finally went for it at the 2000 Gravity Games. He landed but then wiped out while riding away. Hart tried the backflip again at the 2001 X Games but was badly hurt in a fall. Many riders were inspired by Hart's attempts, including Mike Metzger. Metzger was determined to do the backflip. Meanwhile, Travis Pastrana and Hart were working on the trick, too. It soon became a race to see who would successfully pull the move at the 2002 X Games. A month before the Games, Metzger pulled ahead: In front of friends and journalists, he flipped 21 times in a row on jumps in his backyard in California. At the X Games that year, Hart, Pastrana, Metzger, and Kenny Bartram all stuck backflips. But Metzger was the only one to land them back-to-back, a move he called the double fritz, and won the Freestyle gold medal.

NO-FOOTED AIR▶

Although it is a basic freestyle trick, the no-footed air requires solid bike skills, including mastery of simple jumps. Before learning the no-footer, try one-footed airs by launching off a jump, then kicking out your left or right foot. Once you're comfortable with that, go for the no-footer by removing your feet from the pegs while in the air and putting them back on before landing again.

THE CONWAY DAILY SUN/BRUCE BEDFORD/AP

BRIAN SMITH

◀NO-HANDED AIR

A no-hander is tougher than a no-footer because you have to let go of the handlebars for a second — a scary thought for novices. Try one-handed airs first to get the feel. Alternate with one hand and then the other before busting loose and letting both hands free. Remember to grab the bars again before touching down; no-handed landings are a more advanced move.

TIME LINE

1885 Gottlieb Daimler invents the first gas-powered motorcycle by mounting an engine on a wooden bike.

1889 British engineer Joseph Day invents the two-stroke engine, a smaller, lighter, and more powerful alternative to the four-stroke engine used in automobiles.

1903 Harley-Davidson begins making motorcycles in Milwaukee, Wisconsin.

Harley's Here

HARLEY-DAVIDSON ARCHIVES

1924 A motorcycle club in Camberly, England, holds the first scramble on a 2.5-mile cross-country track. Scrambles would evolve into motocross.

LARRY KASPEREK/NEWSPORT

CANCAN▲

Named after a lively French dance where you kick your legs high in the air, the cancan comes from BMX. Cancans are a basic-to-intermediate trick. First, launch your motorcycle in the air, and then kick one leg over the top of the seat to the other side before returning it to the foot pegs. When you're comfortable performing them with your right and left feet, graduate to the two-footed cancan and kick both feet to the same side of the motorcycle.

FAST FACT

The kiss of death is a freestyle motocross move invented by Mike Jones in 2001. While in the air, the rider does a handstand on the handlebars and puts his face close enough to the front tire to kiss it.

957 Motocross grows in pularity in Europe after orld War II, leading to e creation of a world ampionship.

1963 Husqvarna, a Swedish manufacturer, develops lightweight, speedy bikes with two-stroke engines. These are the first motocross models.

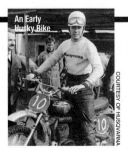

An Early Husky Bike

COURTESY OF HUSQVARNA

1971 The American Motorcyle Association holds the first pro race on a temporary track, at the Daytona International Speedway.

< LEGEND >
JEREMY MCGRATH

Jeremy McGrath was one of the most popular riders of all time. His dominance and style helped fuel the growth of supercross and motocross in the 1990's. McGrath grew up in California racing BMX bikes, but at 15 switched to motorcycles. A quick learner, he turned pro at 17. He showed tremendous promise in the 125cc ranks, winning the Supercross West Region Series in 1991 and 1992. He moved up to the 250cc class in 1993, and won that supercross series as a rookie. By 2000, he had collected a record seven supercross series titles. During that stretch, he also finished in the top three in the motocross series four times, winning it all in 1995. In addition to being famous as a racer, McGrath pioneered freestyle riding by performing a trick called a nacnac while soaring over jumps during races. Nacnacs require kicking one foot behind and across to the other side of the bike. McGrath retired from full-time racing in 2003, and was inducted into the Motorcycle Hall of Fame. In 2004, he won a gold medal in Step Up at the X Games by clearing the best height while jumping his motorcycle. Now 34, he competes in only a few events each year.

JERRY WARD

TIME LINE

1972 The Los Angeles Coliseum hosts a race called the Superbowl of Motocross. The words are combined and "supercross" is born.

"Hurricane" Hannah

C. MOREY/DIGITALPHOTOGRAPHY.TV

1977 Bob "Hurricane" Hannah wins the first of three straight supercross titles, before a skiing accident in 1979 ends his streak.

1981 Mark Barnett wins the supercross championship on a Suzuki motorcyle. No Suzuki rider would win again until Ricky Carmichael in 2005.

NECESSARY OBJECTS

- **MOTORCYCLE:** Motorcycles come in a range of sizes, with loads of features and options. The smallest bikes, for the smallest riders, usually have 50cc engines. From there they go up to 80cc, 100cc, 125cc, 250cc, and 500cc. Each level provides more power. More than half the bikes in the United States have engines smaller than 125cc. You need serious skills to ride anything more powerful.

  Most motorcycles offer choices of clutches, transmissions, and engines (four-stroke or two-stroke). The most common type of transmission requires manual shifting. But beginners may struggle using a manual transmission because you have to switch gears by using the clutch on the handlebars and the shifter near the foot peg. Smaller models for younger riders sometimes offer automatic transmissions.

  To find the right motorcycle for you, visit dealers and have them explain the options on each model. You can save a lot of money by buying a used bike. If you buy from a previous owner, be sure to have a mechanic inspect the bike first. Make sure a mechanic in your area knows how to fix the model you buy. A broken-down bike is as good as no bike at all.

- **HELMET:** After the motorcycle, a helmet is your most important piece of equipment. Motorcycle helmets should cover your entire face with just an opening for your eyes. Fit is important: Helmets should be snug. Motocross helmets have a peak that hangs over the eyes like a visor, and a chinbar that covers the mouth and nose. Look for a sticker inside the helmet that shows that it has been safety-approved by one of these agencies: the Department of Transportation, the Snell Memorial Foundation, or the American National Standards Institute.

- **OTHER EQUIPMENT:** Start with a good pair of boots. That way you can walk away from a crash. Motocross boots provide the most protection. They are knee-high, thick, and stiff, with hard plastic buckles to fasten them tight. It's a good idea to wear goggles to protect your eyes. Also, wear a long-sleeved sweatshirt, jeans, and thin but strong gloves. For extra protection, invest in a chest protector, motocross pants, knee guards, elbow guards, motocross gloves, a neck guard, and a kidney belt.

1982 Donnie Hansen wins the supercross championship, the first for a Honda rider.

Jeff Ward

PAUL BUCKLEY

1985 Jeff Ward wins Kawasaki's first 250cc motocross title.

1988 Rick Johnson wins his second supercross title, the first of nine straight supercross championships by the Honda team.

1991 Jean-Michel Bayle of France becomes the first European to win the AMA Supercross Series title.

Chuck Carothers didn't have a name for his new trick, but he knew it would be awesome if he could land it. Carothers had earned a wild-card invitation to the 2004 X Games because of a video he sent to the selection committee. The footage showed him launching through the air, rolling sideways 360 degrees above his motorcycle, then grabbing on again before landing in a foam pit. Going into the Games, Carothers had never landed the move on dirt. Still, he nailed it on his first run in the Best Trick event. No one could top it, and Carothers won the gold medal. Eventually, he called the trick the Carolla, a combination of his last name and the word "roll." The spin is similar to a body varial, a move riders have been wanting to try for years but have been afraid to attempt. It was such a gnarly move that Carothers thought he could win with it again at the 2005 X Games. But he messed up in midair and wound up slamming hard to the dirt below. If Carothers can come up with another great trick to add to his Carolla, he will be a top FMX rider.

MARK TERRILL/AP

F∆S† FACT

Motocross tracks range from a half-mile to two miles long. Supercross tracks vary in length depending on the size of the arena, but must be at least 20 feet wide. In both motocross and supercross, riders race several laps around the track.

⊢TIME LINE⊢

Crusty Demons

JEFF CROW/ICON SMI

1993 Jeremy McGrath wins the super-cross championship in his first season aboard a 250cc motorcycle. He will go on to win more supercross races than any other rider.

1996 The Crusty Demons Tour begins. Freestyle moto-cross riders pull tricks for enthusiastic crowds across the country.

1997 Jeff Emig beats Jeremy McGrath for the supercross championship, halting McGrath's string of four straight titles.

BRIAN DEEGAN

Like Mike Metzger, Brian Deegan was one of the first motocross racers to make the switch to freestyle riding. Not to be outdone by his buddy, Deegan began working on his own kind of backflip in 2003. Deegan showed the move, an off-axis 360, in the Best Trick event at the 2003 X Games. The off-axis 360 is a backflip done while spinning sideways. It won Deegan a gold medal. It also raised the danger level in freestyle. While trying the trick again over a 90-foot gap at the 2004 Winter X Games, Deegan messed up and fell hard, breaking his leg and both wrists. Although all the top riders today can land backflips, only a few have command of the off-axis 360.

2000 Jeremy McGrath wins his record seventh supercross series title. Ricky Carmichael wins his first 250cc U.S. Motocross Championship. Travis Pastrana wins the 125cc Motocross Championship in his rookie season.

Chad Reed

HEINZ KLUETMEIER

2004 Australian Chad Reed wins the supercross series title while Ricky Carmichael sits out with an injury.

2005 Ricky Carmichael wins his sixth straight AMA 250cc U.S. Motocross Championship and fourth overall supercross title. Travis Pastrana wins his fifth Freestyle gold medal at the X Games.

1 RICKY CARMICHAEL, born November 27, 1979, in Clearwater, Florida. The most dominant motorcycle racer in history, Carmichael is only 26 and already the all-time motocross wins leader. In 2005 he won his sixth straight motocross championship and fourth overall supercross series title. Carmichael is so far ahead, no one may ever catch him.

Ricky Carmichael

2 TRAVIS PASTRANA, born October 8, 1983, in Annapolis, Maryland. A hot amateur national champion in motocross, Pastrana was AMA Motocross/Supercross Rookie of the Year in 2000 after winning the 125cc motocross title. He stepped up to the 250cc class in 2002 but has been grounded by injuries. Meanwhile, Pastrana has been almost unbeatable in freestyle, winning the gold medal at the X Games in five of six tries (1999-2001, 2003, 2005).

3 KEVIN WINDHAM, born February 28, 1978, in Baton Rouge, Louisiana. If not for Carmichael, Windham would own several racing championships. One of the top riders in supercross and motocross over the past eight years, he has finished second for the motocross championship four times (1999, 2001, 2003, 2005). In supercross, he was second in 2004 and third in 2005.

4 BRIAN DEEGAN, born May 9, 1975, in Omaha, Nebraska. The leader of freestyle motocross's bad boys, The Metal Mulisha, Deegan talks tough and backs it up. He has won more X Games medals in motocross than anyone (10), including three golds. He invented the off-axis 360 in 2003. Serious injuries have slowed him lately.

5 NATE ADAMS, born March 29, 1984, in Glendale, Arizona. Smooth and technical, Adams is the only rider to beat Travis Pastrana head-to-head in a freestyle event, topping him for the gold medal at the 2004 X Games. In 2005, Adams added to his five X Games medals with bronze medals in Freestyle and Best Trick. He will be a force in the sport for years to come.

Brian Deegan

6 CHAD REED, born March 15, 1982, in Newcastle, Australia. This aggressive Aussie racer doesn't back down from anyone. He made his debut in the 250cc class in 2003 and placed second in the supercross series and third in motocross. In 2004, he won supercross and finished second in motocross. In 2005, he finished second in supercross.

Chad Reed

SIMON CUDBY

7 KENNY BARTRAM, born August 23, 1978, in Stillwater, Oklahoma. A smooth freestyle rider, Cowboy Kenny is one of the original freestyle stars, with five X Games medals. In 2005, he won gold in Freestyle and bronze in Best Trick at the Gravity Games, silver in Freestyle at the X Games, and finished first in Freestyle Motocross on the Dew Action Sports Tour.

8 JEREMY "TWITCH" STENBERG, born September 27, 1981, in San Diego, California. Stenberg is called "Twitch" because of a tic resulting from Tourette's syndrome. He has tons of talent and a smooth style, but could never seem to put it all together. In 2005, he busted loose, winning Best Trick at the X Games and placing second on the Dew Action Sports Tour. He won Best Trick again at the 2006 X Games.

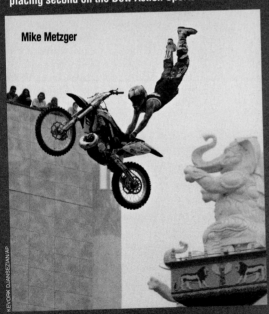

Mike Metzger

KEVORK DJANSEZIAN/AP

9 MIKE METZGER, born November 19, 1975, in Huntington Beach, California. Metzger helped launch freestyle motocross in the early 1990's by pulling BMX tricks during motorcycle races. He cemented his legacy by winning X Games gold in 2002 with the first ever back-to-back backflips. In recent years, Metzger has focused on super moto, a new kind of racing that combines street and dirt tracks.

10 ERNESTO FONSECA, born September 3, 1981, in San Jose, California. Fonseca won the AMA Motocross/Supercross Rookie of the Year Award in 1999, and has been steadily climbing the ranks. In 2005, he finished third in the motocross series and sixth in supercross.

WINTER X GAMES RESULTS

YEAR	EVENT	GOLD	SILVER	BRONZE
2006	Best Trick	Jeremy Stenberg, U.S.	Mat Rebeaud, Switzerland	Ronnie Faisst, U.S.
2005	Best Trick	Brian Deegan, U.S.	Jeff Kargola, U.S.	Dustin Miller, U.S.
2004	Best Trick	Caleb Wyatt, U.S.	Mike Metzger, U.S.	Nate Adams, U.S.
2003	Big Air	Mike Metzger, U.S.	Dane Kinnaird, Australia	Caleb Wyatt, U.S.
2002	Big Air	Brian Deegan, U.S.	Mike Jones, U.S.	Tommy Clowers, U.S.
2001	Big Air	Mike Jones, U.S.	Tommy Clowers, U.S.	Clifford Adoptante, U.S.

SUMMER X GAMES RESULTS

YEAR	EVENT	GOLD	SILVER	BRONZE
2005	Best Trick	Jeremy Stenberg, U.S.	Travis Pastrana, U.S.	Nate Adams, U.S.
2004	Best Trick	Chuck Carothers, U.S.	Nate Adams, U.S.	Travis Pastrana, U.S.
2003	Big Air	Brian Deegan, U.S.	Nate Adams, U.S.	Kenny Bartram, U.S.
2002	Big Air	Mike Metzger, U.S.	Carey Hart, U.S.	Brian Deegan, U.S.
2001	Big Air	Kenny Bartram, U.S.	Dustin Miller, U.S.	Brian Deegan, U.S.
2005	Freestyle	Travis Pastrana, U.S.	Kenny Bartram, U.S.	Nate Adams, U.S.
2004	Freestyle	Nate Adams, U.S.	Travis Pastrana, U.S.	Adam Jones, U.S.
2003	Freestyle	Travis Pastrana, U.S.	Nate Adams, U.S.	Brian Deegan, U.S.
2002	Freestyle	Mike Metzger, U.S.	Kenny Bartram, U.S.	Drake McElroy, U.S.
2001	Freestyle	Travis Pastrana, U.S.	Clifford Adoptante, U.S.	Jake Windham, U.S.
2000	Freestyle	Travis Pastrana, U.S.	Tommy Clowers, U.S.	Brian Deegan, U.S.
1999	Freestyle	Travis Pastrana, U.S.	Mike Cinqmars, U.S.	Brian Deegan, U.S.
2005	Step Up	Tommy Clowers, U.S.	Matt Buyten, U.S.	Jeremy McGrath, U.S.
2004	Step Up	Jeremy McGrath, U.S.	Matt Buyten, U.S.	Tommy Clowers, U.S.
2003	Step Up	Matt Buyten, U.S.	Tommy Clowers, U.S.	Ronnie Renner, U.S.
2002	Step Up	Tommy Clowers, U.S.	Mike Metzger, U.S.	Brian Deegan, U.S.
2001	Step Up	Tommy Clowers, U.S.	Travis Pastrana, U.S.	Colin Morrison, U.S.(tie) Ronnie Renner, U.S. Kris Rourke, U.S. Jeremy Stenberg, U.S.
2000	Step Up	Tommy Clowers, U.S.	Kris Rourke, U.S.	Brian Deegan, U.S.
2005	Super Moto	Doug Henry, U.S.	Jeremy McGrath, U.S.	Chad Reed, U.S.
2004	Super Moto	Ben Bostrom, U.S.	Eddy Seel, Belgium	Jeremy McGrath, U.S.

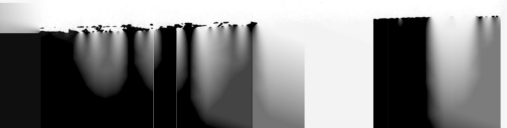

SUMMER GRAVITY GAMES RESULTS

YEAR	EVENT	GOLD	SILVER	BRONZE
2005	Freestyle	Kenny Bartram, U.S.	Jeremy Stenberg, U.S.	Ronnie Renner, U.S.
2004	Freestyle	Nate Adams, U.S.	Jeremy Stenberg, U.S.	Ronnie Faisst, U.S.
2003	Freestyle	Nate Adams, U.S.	Travis Pastrana, U.S.	Ronnie Renner, U.S.
2002	Freestyle	Travis Pastrana, U.S.	Mike Metzger, U.S.	Kenny Bartram, U.S.
2001	Freestyle	Travis Pastrana, U.S.	Clifford Adoptante, U.S.	Tommy Clowers, U.S.
2000	Freestyle	Brian Deegan, U.S.	Mike Metzger, U.S.	Kenny Bartram, U.S.
1999	Freestyle	Travis Pastrana, U.S.	Brian Deegan, U.S.	Carey Hart, U.S.

DEW ACTION SPORTS TOUR RESULTS

YEAR	EVENT	GOLD	SILVER	BRONZE
2005	FMX	Kenny Bartram, U.S.	Jeremy Stenberg, U.S.	Mike Mason, U.S.

AMA MOTOCROSS CHAMPIONSHIP RESULTS

YEAR	EVENT	GOLD	SILVER	BRONZE
2005	250 Class	Ricky Carmichael, U.S.	Kevin Windham, U.S.	Ernesto Fonseca, U.S.
2004	250 Class	Ricky Carmichael, U.S.	Chad Reed, Australia	Kevin Windham, U.S.
2003	250 Class	Ricky Carmichael, U.S.	Kevin Windham, U.S.	Chad Reed, Australia
2002	250 Class	Ricky Carmichael, U.S.	Timmy Ferry, U.S.	Ezra Lusk, U.S.
2001	250 Class	Ricky Carmichael, U.S.	Kevin Windham, U.S.	Timmy Ferry, U.S.

AMA SUPERCROSS CHAMPIONSHIP RESULTS

YEAR	EVENT	GOLD	SILVER	BRONZE
2005	250 Class	Ricky Carmichael, U.S.	Chad Reed, Australia	Kevin Windham, U.S.
2004	250 Class	Chad Reed, Australia	Kevin Windham, U.S.	Mike LaRocco, U.S.
2003	250 Class	Ricky Carmichael, U.S.	Chad Reed, U.S.	Ernesto Fonseca, U.S.
2002	250 Class	Ricky Carmichael, U.S.	David Vuillemin, France	Jeremy McGrath, U.S.
2001	250 Class	Ricky Carmichael, U.S.	Jeremy McGrath, U.S.	Mike LaRocco, U.S.

TOP 10 PLACES TO RIDE

1 LORETTA LYNN'S RANCH, HURRICANE MILLS, TENNESSEE. A sprawling ranch owned by the famous country singer, the grounds feature a plantation house, campground, concert venue, and of course, a top motocross track that hosts the annual amateur national championships.

Loretta Lynn's Ranch

2 SANDS OF SOUTHWICK, SOUTHWICK, MASSACHUSETTS. This track winds through rolling, wooded hills. It is known as one of the tougher tracks in the sport, due to its ruts and shifting sands. It hosts the Southwick Motocross National each year.

3 CASTILLO RANCH, LOS ALAMOS, CALIFORNIA. The natural terrain of rolling hills, cliffs, and hips makes it perfect for huge air. The Ranch also has two tracks — supercross and motocross — and multiple freestyle ramps. Riders rave about the loamy dirt. This kind of dirt makes the best riding surface because it doesn't clump and is great for sliding.

4 TRAVIS PASTRANA'S HOUSE, ANNAPOLIS, MARYLAND. Pastrana has a BMX and a freestyle course, plus a trampoline and a foam pit, for him and his friends to learn the latest tricks. He also has a full-size motocross track.

5 COOPERLAND, STILLWATER, OKLAHOMA. Cooperland has two tracks — a peewee and a larger professional-sized course with numerous tabletops, steep terrain, and a deep, wooded ravine. The loam and red-clay dirt conditions are ideal.

MIKE BASHER

Cooperland

Metal Mulisha Compound

SIMON CUDBY

6 MILLSAPS TRAINING FACILITY, CAIRO, GEORGIA. This motocross training facility lets aspiring pros get their hands — and everything else — dirty. Millsaps has four tracks: motocross, supercross, arenacross, and peewee. Add in its shop, lounge, RV park, game room, clubhouse, and full-time mechanic, and what more could a rider want?

7 THE METAL MULISHA COMPOUND, TEMECULA, CALIFORNIA. The compound is located at the home of motocross bad-boy Brian Deegan, who heads The Metal Mulisha, a crew of tattooed, hard-core freestyle riders. The Mulisha's 22 riders — including "Twitch" Stenberg, Ronnie Faisst, and Deegan — polish their moves on the freestyle course and foam pit.

8 DUMONT DUNES, BAKER, CALIFORNIA. This 8,000-acre sea of sand in Southern California makes for off-road bliss. Surrounded by steep volcanic hills, Dumont has rolling dunes, with some as high as 500 feet. The only drawback is that the area is low-lying and gets hot!

9 LOMMEL, BELGIUM. This is a famous sand track in the country of Belgium, with a tradition of producing top local talent and drawing great crowds.

10 SPRING CREEK MOTOCROSS PARK, MILLVILLE, MINNESOTA. Motorcycles have been raced at Spring Creek for 40 years. Its track layout is great for spectators.

CHAPTER 4

SKATEBOARDING

Skateboarding was born in Southern
California as an activity surfers did
when the waves were flat.

Tony Hawk is the sport's
greatest and most
famous rider.

GRANT BRITTAIN

Skateboarding emerged in the 1950's, riding the popularity of surfing. The earliest skateboards had homemade decks cut from planks of wood with steel roller-skate wheels and trucks (the axles that hold the wheels to the board). When waves were flat, Southern California surfers cruised the sidewalks on these primitive boards.

The Roller Derby roller-skate company saw the potential of this new activity and made the first mass-produced skateboard in 1959. During the early 1960's, skateboarding continued to feed off of surfing's popularity. By 1963, the first pro skateboard competition was held in Hermosa Beach, California.

Off and Rolling

At the same time, Larry Stevenson, the publisher of *Surf Guide*, a surfing magazine, created what he called the first pro skateboards under his brand, Makaha. These boards were the first to use clay wheels, which were cheaper to produce than steel wheels. Stevenson formed a team of riders to tour the country and promote his boards. Surfing was still a huge influence, and several of the skaters rode barefoot — flowing and carving as if they were on a surfboard. The most progressive skaters performed nose wheelies, jumps, and handstands.

Skateboarding grew rapidly. In 1964, two companies, Hobie (surfboards) and Vita Pakt (juice), teamed up to start Hobie Skateboards. The following year, *The Quarterly Skateboarder* began publication. (The magazine would later be renamed *SkateBoarder.*) But just as skateboarding appeared ready to take off, the sport took a nosedive. The cause: a combination of poor equipment and poor publicity. Clay wheels would stop suddenly when they hit a crack or a stone, sending the rider flying. Skaters were getting injured, and communities banned skateboarding as a dangerous activity. This was a disaster for the sport. The number of skateboarders shrank and skateboarding went underground for the next decade.

MIKE BLABAC

Danny Way invented the Mega Ramp and Big Air riding.

Reinventing the Wheel

The next wave of skating popularity arrived in the mid-1970's, again because of improvements in equipment. In 1970, a surfer named Frank Nasworthy began experimenting with urethane wheels to replace clay models. Nasworthy introduced Cadillac Wheels in 1973. It was soon obvious that they provided better traction and a smoother ride. Truck manufacturers also began designing axles strictly for skateboards. Precision bearings, which are placed inside the wheels and allow the wheels to roll more easily, produced a faster, smoother ride. Skateboarding was ready for a comeback.

Bob Burnquist has won 10 X Games medals.

FA$T FACT

Switch stance is when a rider stands on a board with what would normally be his back foot in front. Performing tricks "switch" is difficult. Extra points are awarded for riding this way in contests.

The Z-Boys

Meanwhile, a group of Southern California skaters, known as the Z-Boys, pioneered tricks that led to a growing movement toward vertical (or vert) skating. Concrete skateparks began to open across the country. By 1976, new equipment had developed for the new terrain: Boards went from 7 inches wide to 9 inches wide. On these larger, more stable boards, early stars such as Tony Alva, Jay Adams, and Stacy Peralta invented radical vertical tricks.

Two of the biggest advances in tricks occurred in 1978. Alan Gelfand invented the ollie, a no-handed aerial. Alva became the first skater to be featured in the pages of *SkateBoarder* doing an aerial, which showed him pulling a frontside air. Suddenly, skating was all about getting airborne.

The Sport Crashes

The popularity of aerials and skateparks eventually caused the sport to crash yet again in the early 1980's. High insurance costs forced skatepark owners to close down. Discouraged, many skaters dropped out of the sport. Skateboarding went underground again, except for skaters who built their own halfpipes (vert ramps) to replace the skateparks. Skateboarding began to be associated with the punk music movement because of their similar do-it-yourself, rebel attitude. In 1981, *Thrasher* magazine was started, combining coverage of skating and music.

The Hawk Lands

Some great skaters developed despite the down period. Fourteen-year-old Tony Hawk won his first contest at the Del Mar Skate Ranch in California in 1982. By 1983, skateboarding again began to grow in popularity due to the backyard vert ramp scene.

In 1984, the skateboarding company Powell Peralta debuted the first skate video, *The Bones Brigade Video Show*. Created by former pro and Z-Boys member Stacy Peralta, the video showcased the talents of Hawk, Steve Caballero, Lance Mountain, Mike McGill, and Rodney Mullen. The video's popularity fed a surge of interest in the sport.

Taking to the Streets

At the same time, Hawk's father, Frank, founded the National Skateboard Association (NSA), a nationwide contest series. Two of the NSA's biggest vert stars were Hawk and Christian Hosoi. Their differing styles — Hawk was technical, Hosoi went huge — led to legendary battles in national contests. Although vert skating ruled, some innovative riders, such as Natas Kaupas and Mark Gonzales, began to take the sport away from vert ramps and to the streets. They experimented with ollies and riding handrails. Meanwhile, Mullen ruled freestyle, a flatland discipline in which skaters did wheelies and handstands. He revolutionized this type of skating with his ability to invent tricks in which he flipped his board with his feet. Mullen linked these new moves together, creating amazing combinations. His style was the foundation for modern street skating.

Bye-Bye Freestyle

By the late 1980's, skateboarding was about to undergo major changes. Some pros rejected established brands and started their own companies. These companies, owned by street and freestyle skaters, created smaller boards and wheels. Upturned noses on decks became standard. The equipment changes placed more of an emphasis on street skating, which required lighter, more maneuverable boards.

The improvements in equipment spurred a greater interest in street skating — and led to a backlash against vert. Eventually freestyle died out altogether. Skateboarding dipped in popularity again during the early 1990's.

Skateboarding's New Heights

By the mid-1990's, however, skateboarding was ready for its next — and biggest — boom. The start of it all was ESPN's Extreme Games (later renamed the X Games), first held in Providence, Rhode Island, in 1995. The TV format brought skateboarding to a wider audience and made stars of many skaters, including Andy Macdonald, Bob Burnquist, and Chris Senn. Hawk especially benefited from his success at the X Games, and his popularity soared. His status grew even more when he landed the first 900 (2½ rotations) at the 1999 X Games. That same year, Activision released the first edition of what would become a video-game franchise, *Tony Hawk's Pro Skater*. Now in its eighth version, Hawk's game is one of the bestselling video games of all time and has helped introduce skating to an ever-larger audience.

A New Image

Following the success of the X Games, other organizations created large televised contests, such as the Gravity Games and the Dew Action Sports Tour. The professional presentation of the events and the fan-friendly attitude of the riders helped reshape people's impression of skaters. Thanks to skateboarding's new, positive image, more parents supported their kids' involvement. Communities nationwide built skateparks, allowing more people to experience skating.

Skateboarding continues to head in new, exciting directions. In 2003, Danny Way built the first Mega Ramp, a 64-foot-tall structure that launched him more than 70 feet over a gap and more than 20 feet above a 27-foot quarterpipe. Nothing of such size and scale had ever been done in the sport before, and Way's stunts have been hugely popular. In July 2005, Way used a Mega Ramp to launch over a 44-foot-high, 70-foot-long section of the Great Wall of China. Images of the skater soaring over the Great Wall were printed in newspapers around the world. The pictures symbolized how far skateboarding had come in 50 years — from a wacky activity for Southern California surfers to a sport recognized worldwide.

Eric Koston is a master of street skating.

ATIBA JEFFERSON

INNOVATOR

DANNY WAY

Danny Way has been pushing skateboarding into new territory since he turned pro in 1988 at age 14. He was a talented young skater who helped bring street-style flip tricks (flipping the board in midair) onto vert ramps. Because of that, he was named Skater of the Year by *Thrasher* magazine in 1991. In 1994, Way suffered serious neck and back injuries while surfing; the injuries kept him off his skateboard for a year. He returned to his fearless ways in 1997 by jumping out of a helicopter onto a vert ramp. Way's hard-charging style had serious consequences: From 1999 to 2002, he underwent seven operations, including five on his knees. After he healed, Way pulled his biggest stunt yet. He built the first Mega Ramp with help from DC Shoes, the skate shoe company he cofounded. The ramp was a 64-foot-tall monster that launched him across a 75-foot gap at a speed of 40 miles per hour onto another section of the ramp. It gave him the momentum to pull huge airs above a 27-foot-high quarterpipe. His jumps were filmed for *The DC Video*, which was released in 2003. The video — and the jumps — rocked the skateboarding world. The following year, the X Games added a Mega Ramp and created a new event, Big Air. Way won the gold medal at the Games while setting a new distance record of 79 feet. *Thrasher* again named him Skater of the Year, the only rider ever to be honored twice. In 2005, Way used a Mega Ramp to launch himself 70 feet over a portion of the Great Wall of China.

< LEGEND >
RODNEY MULLEN

Without Rodney Mullen's dedication and creativity, modern street skating would not be what it is today. Mullen started as a freestyle skater in Gainesville, Florida, in 1977. Freestyle was a popular flatland discipline in which skaters performed tricks such as handstands, wheelies, and spins.

After only nine months of skating, Mullen got a sponsorship from a local surf shop. In 1980, a 13-year-old Mullen turned pro for the prestigious Powell Peralta team and began a 10-year run of contest dominance. During this time, he won all but one competition — approximately 40 wins by his estimation — using dozens of tricks that he invented.

In 1989, Mullen left Powell Peralta to help found the skateboard company World Industries with pro Steve Rocco. Mullen developed smaller decks with upturned noses, along with other equipment innovations. These changes aided the boom in street skating by offering gear that was lighter and made doing tricks easier. By the early 1990's, freestyle

skating was dying due to a lack of interest. Mullen switched to street skating, showing his stunning footwork and flip tricks in the skate video *Questionable*. At age 39, he continues to invent and impress in his trick battles with Daewon Song in the classic *Rodney vs. Daewon* video series.

GRANT BRITTAIN

THE 900

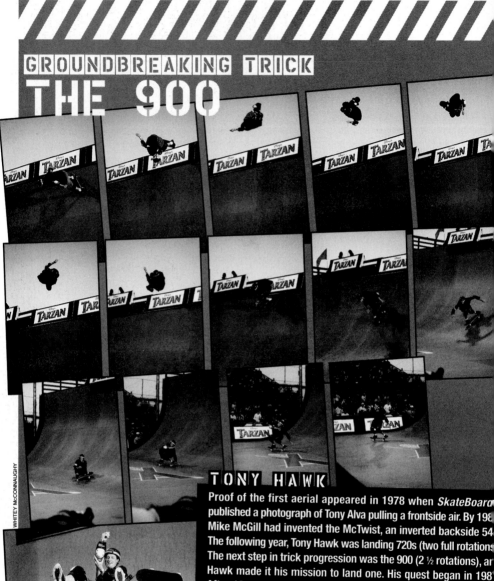

WHITEY McCONNAUGHY

TONY HAWK

Proof of the first aerial appeared in 1978 when *SkateBoard* published a photograph of Tony Alva pulling a frontside air. By 198 Mike McGill had invented the McTwist, an inverted backside 54 The following year, Tony Hawk was landing 720s (two full rotations The next step in trick progression was the 900 (2 ½ rotations), an Hawk made it his mission to land one. His quest began in 198 After 10 years and many failed tries, he finally set a timetabl Capture the 900 on film for his 1998 skate video, *The End*. Ala Hawk missed his deadline. But one year later, at the 1999 X Game he tried again during the Vert Best Trick competition. Although tin had expired on his session, Hawk kept going. He attempted 1 unsuccessful 900s while the crowd and other skaters watched Finally, Hawk spun 2 ½ times, landed low, and rode away. His hand went up and his fellow skaters mobbed him on the ramp t celebrate the historic moment. Six years later, only a few skater have joined him in the 900 club.

NECESSARY OBJECTS

● **SKATEBOARD:** Skateboard decks are made of seven layers of plywood glued together for strength and flexibility. They generally range from 7½ to 8¼ inches wide and 31 to 32½ inches long. A wider deck is better for taller skaters and vert riding, while a smaller deck is better for smaller skaters and street riding. Trucks, the metal axles attached to the deck and wheels, allow the board to turn. Truck size should be within ¼ inch of the width of the deck. Then there are the wheels. Two considerations are size and hardness. Most wheels come in sizes ranging from 48 to 65 millimeters. Bigger wheels are better for vert riding, while smaller ones are lighter and better for street tricks. Wheel hardness usually ranges from 95a to 99a — the higher the number, the harder the wheel. Softer wheels are better for rough surfaces, like streets, and offer more traction. Harder wheels are smoother and faster, but perform poorly on imperfect surfaces. Bearings are the final part of the setup. They are tiny steel or ceramic balls in a metal casing that are fitted into the hollow section of the wheels and allow them to roll more easily. The Annular Bearing Engineering Committee (ABEC) rates bearings for quality. They are based on the following scale: ABEC 1, ABEC 3, ABEC 5, ABEC 7, and ABEC 9. Although ABEC 1 bearings are basic, they are good enough for most skaters.

● **HELMET:** The helmet is probably the most important piece of equipment after the skateboard. A blow to the head will end a fun skate session in a hurry. Not all helmets are created equal. They should be rated by the U.S. Consumer Product Safety Commission (CPSC). Helmets first appeared in the 1970's and were required at concrete skateparks. Today, pro street skaters are often pictured in skateboard magazines without helmets, but vert skaters almost always wear them because of the danger of falling while riding a large ramp or pool. Amateur riders — street or vert — should always wear a helmet.

● **PADS:** Skaters started using pads during the 1970's because skateparks often required them. The earliest versions resembled volleyball pads, with soft shells. But given the rough concrete surface of most skateparks, something more durable and protective was needed. Rector was the first company to market plastic-capped skateboard pads for the knees, elbows, and wrists. Street skaters today are seldom seen using pads, but vert

TIME LINE

1950'S When they are not riding waves, surfers in Southern California start riding on planks of wood with roller-skate wheels attached.

COURTESY OF JIM FITZPATRICK

An early board

1959 Roller Derby, a manufacturer of roller skates, creates the first mass-produced skateboard with steel wheels.

1962 Larry Stevenson, publisher of *Surf Guide*, founds the Makaha Skateboard Company, the first company to create pro models, which have skaters' names on them.

THE BASIC TRICKS

BOARDSLIDE▶

A boardslide can be performed on curbs, handrails, vert ramps, and ledges. The skater approaches the sliding surface with speed and does an ollie, or for low surfaces, simply turns the board about 90 degrees in either direction. The part of the deck between the trucks meets the edge of the curb, handrail, ramp, or ledge. The skater plants his feet firmly for balance and the board slides along the surface's edge.

ATIBA JEFFERSON

TONY DONALDSON/ICON SMI

◀MANUAL

A manual is also called a wheelie, which has been a standard skateboarding move since the sport's earliest days. A skater puts weight on the tail end of the board and pops the front wheels into the air. True manuals require landing an ollie in a wheelie and holding it until performing another maneuver. The move requires excellent balance and footwork.

⊢TIME LINE⊢

1963 The first skateboard contest is held at Pier Avenue Junior High School in Hermosa Beach, California.

1964 Hobie, the surfboard manufacturer, begins making skateboards.

Hobie
skateboard

COURTESY OF HOBIE

1965 The first skate magazine, *The Quarterly Skateboarder*, is founded.

DAVE MIRRA

He's called "Miracle Boy," but there's nothing miraculous about Mirra's riding. He is the dominant BMX stunt rider of the past 10 years — and the favorite to win any contest he enters. Mirra is a master of both vert and park. He has won more medals (19) than any athlete in X Games history.

LYN-Z ADAMS HAWKINS

No terrain — streets, ramps, or bowls — is safe from skateboarder Hawkins's attack. In 2004, she won the gold medal in women's Vert at the X Games and the bronze medal in Street at the Gravity Games. She was just 14 years old. In 2005, Hawkins snared the silver in Vert at the X Games.

HANNAH TETER

Teter is the younger sister of two pro snowboarders, Abe and Elijah. The Teters are known for huge airs, but 19-year-old Hannah does more than just go big. In 2003, she was one of the first women to land a 900 (2 ½ rotations) in halfpipe competition. The same year, Teter placed third in Superpipe at the Winter X Games and third in Halfpipe and Slopestyle at the U.S. Open. In 2004, she earned gold in Superpipe at the Winter X Games. But Teter reached the high point of her career when she won the gold medal in Halfpipe at the 2006 Winter Olympics.

MAT HOFFMAN

Nicknamed "The Condor" for his ability to soar, Hoffman set a world record in 2001 with a 26 ½-foot-high air above a 24-foot ramp. He is the first rider to land tricks such as the flair and the 900 — and is credited with inventing more than 50 others. Hoffman retired from competition in 2002 as a legend known for his toughness.

TANNER HALL

Hall has unmatched all-around skiing skills. His hard-charging approach in Superpipe and Slopestyle has caused legions of young freestyle skiers to imitate him. He is a three-time Winter X Games gold medalist in Slopestyle (2002-04). But Hall is just as comfortable in a pipe as he is in the backcountry, where his stunts show that he's more than just a contest rider.

ANDY IRONS

Irons is a three-time Association of Surfing Professionals (ASP) World Tour champion (2002-04). He has beaten the best, including the legendary Kelly Slater, and ranks among the all-time greats of the sport. At age 27, Irons is one of only four surfers to have won three or more world championships in the tour's 30-year history.

DANNY WAY

In 2003, Way launched from a 64-foot-tall Mega Ramp and soared 75 feet through the air, creating a new discipline in skateboarding called Big Air. The event debuted the next year at the X Games — and Way won the gold medal, of course. For an encore, he jumped a section of the Great Wall of China and repeated as X Games Big Air champ in 2005.

DALLAS FRIDAY

Friday has been at the top of women's wakeboarding since turning pro as a 13-year-old in 2000. She has won more X Games medals (6) than any other female wakeboarder, including gold the past three years (2003, 2004, and 2005).

RICKY CARMICHAEL

No rider has ruled motor sports as completely as Carmichael has. In 2005, he won his sixth straight national motocross title and his fourth career supercross title. Carmichael is only 25 years old, but he already has more than twice as many career motocross race wins as any rider in history.

BLAIR MORGAN

Morgan has won a medal in SnoCross at every Winter X Games since 1999, including five golds (2001-03, 2005-06). Add in his 12 national championships, and the native of Prince Albert, Saskatchewan, Canada, has the hardware to prove he's the world's top sled jockey.

GRETCHEN BLEILER

Bleiler's signature move is the crippler, an inverted 540-degree spin. Bleiler has been one of the top women's halfpipe riders for the past several years. In 2003 and 2005, she won the Superpipe event at the Winter X Games and the Halfpipe event at the U.S. Open. She won the silver medal in Halfpipe at the 2006 Winter Olympics.

EITO AND TAKESHI YASUTOKO

The Yasutoko brothers, Eito, 23, *(top)* and Takeshi, 20, learned their moves at their dad's skatepark in Kobe, Japan. They arrived in North America in 1998, and even though they barely spoke English, blew away the competition. Together, they have won 12 X Games medals. In any language, the Yasutokos are awesome.

BRIAN DEEGAN

Deegan is the leader of the Metal Mulisha, a crew of hard-core, tattooed freestyle motocross riders. But Deegan is the most decorated of them all: He has the most X Games medals (9) of any motocross rider. Deegan's fearless approach has led to many injuries, including a slam in May 2005 that required the removal of a kidney.

KELLY SLATER

Slater is the greatest surfer in the world. He got his start in Cocoa Beach, Florida, riding waves with a mastery and style never seen before. Slater won six ASP World Tour championships in seven years (1992 and 1994-98). He retired at age 26, but returned to the tour in 2002 and won a record seventh title in 2005.

SHAUN WHITE

White turned pro at age 12. Since then, he's been like an avalanche — an unstoppable force on a mountain. Now 19, he has won eight Winter X Games medals in Slopestyle and Superpipe, including six gold. The board-sports prodigy is a pro skateboarder, too — he won the silver medal in Vert at the 2005 X Games. He also won gold in Halfpipe at the 2006 Winter Olympics.

FABIOLA DA SILVA

This Brazilian is the face of women's inline skating. Da Silva has won seven gold medals in nine years of competing at the X Games. When the women's competition was phased out in 2004, she competed against the men, finishing sixth.

PHILLIP SOVEN

The 17-year-old rider known as "Froggy" has an awesome future ahead of him. In 2004, Soven ranked fourth on the Pro Wakeboard Tour and won the gold medal at the X Games. In 2005, he finished fourth on the pro tour again, earned silver at the X Games, and took gold at the Gravity Games.

TRAVIS PASTRANA

Pastrana made quite a splash at the 1999 X Games. After securing the gold medal in Freestyle Motocross, the then-15-year-old launched his motorcycle into San Francisco Bay to celebrate. It was the first of three straight freestyle gold medals at the X Games. Always a crowd favorite, Pastrana has also raced pro motocross and supercross, but lately has focused on rally car racing.

JOE KROLICK

OLLIE ▲

The ollie is a no-handed aerial. It was invented by and named for Alan "Ollie" Gelfand in 1978. The move was first performed on vert. In the ramp, a skater must bend his knees and allow the board to pop away from the lip, then turn 180 degrees before landing. An ollie on the street, first done by Rodney Mullen in 1981, is performed slightly differently. The skater crouches on the board and thrusts his rear foot downward to slap the tail against the ground. He quickly jumps, allowing his front foot to gently guide the board's upward direction before leveling off and then pushing both feet downward for an even landing.

₹97| Larry Stevenson, ʋnder of Makaha ꜱateboards, invents ꜱd patents the first ꜱktail, the upturned ꜱction on the tail of a ꜱck.

1973 Clay wheels become history when Frank Nasworthy begins selling Cadillac Wheels, the first urethane skateboard wheels.

Peggy Oki, a Z-Boy

PAT DARRIN/SONY PICTURES CLASSICS

1975 The Zephyr skate team, known as the Z-Boys, debuts at the Bahne-Cadillac Skateboard Championship in Del Mar, California. The team's style and attitude help usher in vertical skating, which will dominate the sport for the next 15 years.

<GREATEST MOMENT>
TONY ALVA'S AERIAL

Tony Alva was a surfer who took up skateboarding during the early 1970's. He was from a section of Santa Monica, California, called Dogtown. Alva and a group of other skaters, also from Dogtown, became part of a skate team for the Zephyr surf shop. The team was called the Z-Boys. At the time, most skateboarding was performed on flat surfaces, and many tricks consisted of gymnastic moves such as handstands. The Z-Boys brought a new style to skating. They began riding banked walls on their boards in an attempt to practice their surfing moves. Eventually, they realized that the shape of an empty swimming pool resembled the curved face of a wave. Alva and the Z-Boys began riding pools, carving near the lip. Soon they began getting two wheels above the lip, then three. Finally, Alva busted loose. He rode up the wall and flew briefly above the lip before coming down again. No one knows for sure when the first aerial was performed, but a photo of Alva pulling a frontside air was the first picture of an aerial ever published. It was seen in the January 1978 issue of *SkateBoarder*. By that time Alva was already a skating legend, having won the world professional overall title in 1977, the same year he founded Alva Skateboard Company.

GLEN E. FRIEDMAN/SONY PICTURES CLASSICS

TIME LINE

1976 The first skate shoe arrives when the Vans shoe company designs a blue-and-red model with Z-Boys Tony Alva and Stacy Peralta.

1978 Alan "Ollie" Gelfand perfects a no-handed aerial, and the ollie is born. A photograph of Tony Alva pulling a frontside air, the first of its kind, appears in *SkateBoarder*.

1982 Fourteen-year-old Tony Hawk turns pro for Powell Peralta and wins his first contest.

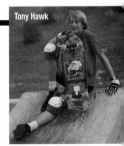

Tony Hawk

Ryan Sheckler, age 16, has been rising through the skating ranks since he got his first sponsor at age seven. He turned pro at age 13, in 2003. Four months later, he rocked the contest scene, becoming the youngest athlete to win a gold medal, in Park, at the X Games. Sheckler was no longer just some little kid who could skate, but a true pro with moves that could beat the best. He cooled off in 2004, but came back to win the inaugural Dew Cup in Street on the 2005 Dew Action Sports Tour.

COURTESY OF TRANSWORLD SKATEBOARDING

F A S T FACT
The McTwist is a standard vert move. It is an inverted backside 540-degree (1½-rotation) spin. Powell Peralta Bones Brigade member Mike McGill debuted the move in 1984.

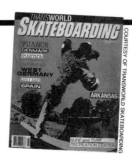

COURTESY OF TRANSWORLD SKATEBOARDING

983 *Transworld Skateboarding* begins publishing as a reaction to *Thrasher*, and offers a positive message: Skate and Create.

1984 The first skate video, *The Bones Brigade Video Show*, debuts. It features the Powell Peralta team.

1986 Pros Natas Kaupas and Mark Gonzales begin riding handrails in city streets.

GROUNDBREAKING TRICK
GREAT WALL JUMP

DANNY WAY

Danny Way has jumped out of a helicopter onto a vert ramp twice, in 1997 and 1999. He has set records for the highest air. But the stunt he dreamed up in 2003 took skateboarding in a whole new direction. With help from DC Shoes, Way had a 64-foot-tall Mega Ramp built in the desert in Southern California. It was nine stories high and stretched longer than a football field. It included a 70-foot gap and a 27-foot-tall quarterpipe at the end. Way rode it in secret, setting Guinness records in distance (75 feet) and height above a ramp (23½ feet). The following year, he gave the X Games permission to build a Mega Ramp. It was used for a new discipline called Big Air. Way won a gold medal in the event and set a new distance world record (79 feet). Still, he had bigger goals in mind. On July 9, 2005, Way rode a Mega Ramp that launched him over a 44-foot-tall, 70-foot-long section of the Great Wall of China, called the Ju Yong Guan Gate *(above)*. It's hard to imagine anyone topping Way's stunt, except maybe Way himself.

MIKE BLABAC

TIME LINE

1988 Danny Way, age 14, turns pro for H-Street.

1995 ESPN's Extreme Games are held in Providence, Rhode Island. They are renamed the X Games the next year.

COURTESY OF ACTIVISION

1999 Tony Hawk lands the first 900, at the X Games. Activision releases *Tony Hawk's Pro Skater* for PlayStation.

<UP−AND−COMER>
LYN-Z ADAMS HAWKINS

Lyn-Z Adams Hawkins first dropped in on a vert ramp at age 10 because she wanted to be like her older brother. Now, many skaters want to be like her. Hawkins can rip on the street, halfpipe, or in the pool. At the 2003 X Games, the then-13-year-old won a silver medal in Park and a bronze medal in Vert. The following year, she won bronze in Street at the Gravity Games and gold in Vert at the X Games, where she became the first woman to land a kickflip indy. In 2005, she snared a silver medal in Vert at the X Games. Expect her to dominate women's skateboarding for years to come.

SCOTT POMMIER/TRANSWORLD SKATEBOARDING

FA$T FACT

Although Tony Hawk has been semiretired from competition since 1999, he still holds the record for most X Games medals by a skateboarder (16).

2002 Tony Hawk's Boom Boom HuckJam tour hits the road, bringing skateboarding and other action sports to arenas across the United States.

2003 Danny Way debuts the Mega Ramp in *The DC Video* to much acclaim. The ramp is added to the X Games the next year in a new event called Big Air.

2005 Danny Way uses a Mega Ramp to launch over a section of the Great Wall of China.

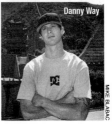

Danny Way

MIKE BLABAC

TOP 10 ATHLETES

1 DANNY WAY, born April 15, 1974, in Portland, Oregon. Way is a creative and gutsy skater. He rides all terrain but is best known for vert and the Mega Ramp, which he invented. Way is the only skater to be named Skater of the Year by *Thrasher* magazine twice (1991 and 2004). He holds Guinness World Records for distance and height. Way's biggest contribution to skateboarding is the Mega Ramp and the discipline it launched, Big Air, in which he is undefeated.

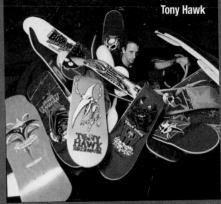

Tony Hawk

2 TONY HAWK, born May 12, 1968, in San Diego, California. Hawk is the greatest vert skater of all time. He won 73 of an estimated 103 competitions he entered during his 17-year career. Hawk also invented many tricks, including the 720, the 900, and the kickflip McTwist. Though he's semiretired from competition, he is still among the world's best ramp riders and an unofficial ambassador for skateboarding.

Paul Rodriguez

3 PAUL RODRIGUEZ, born December 31, 1984, in Northridge, California. "P-Rod" is the smoothest, most consistent street skater around. He is the son of comedian Paul Rodriguez, but there's nothing funny about Junior's style. Rodriguez is a serious success on the contest scene, winning X Games gold in Street in 2004 and 2005.

4 BUCKY LASEK, born December 3, 1972, in Baltimore, Maryland. A longtime pro, Lasek is a smooth and technical ramp rider. During his 15-year career, he has won just about every major contest once. He has more X Games gold medals in Vert (4) than any other skater. At age 33, Lasek is still on top of his game: In 2005, he won Vert at the Gravity Games and at the inaugural Dew Cup on the Dew Action Sports Tour.

5 PIERRE-LUC GAGNON, born May 2, 1980, in Montreal, Quebec, Canada. The French Canadian is fluent in all languages of the ramp. He can work the lip, pull technical tricks, and go big with spins on the Mega Ramp. PLG's vert runs are known for his use of the entire ramp and his mind-blowing moves. In 2005, he won gold in Vert, silver in Big Air, and bronze in Vert Best Trick at the X Games. It was his second triple-medal performance in two years.

6 BOB BURNQUIST, born October 10, 1976, in Rio de Janeiro, Brazil. Burnquist is famous for his switch stance and laid-back personality. He is always inventing new variations for lip and flip tricks. The Brazilian has won 10 X Games medals, including 4 gold. In 2005, he won Vert Best Trick at the X Games for the gnar jar, a frontside 540 nose grab.

7 ERIC KOSTON, born April 29, 1975, in Bangkok, Thailand. Koston is a long-time ruler of street skating. He is part of an older generation of street skaters who raised the level of technical skating with style. Koston is respected as an all-around master by the core skating community and has become well known to the public after winning six X Games medals, including three golds.

Daewon Song

8 DAEWON SONG, born February 19, 1975, in Seoul, Korea. Song is a technical and stunt wizard. He awes fans and other skaters with dangerously complicated tricks, including launching an ollie from the roof of one building to another. Song's trick battles against Rodney Mullen in the *Rodney vs. Daewon* video series are the stuff of legend. *Transworld Skateboarding* named him Street Skater of the Year in 2005.

9 CHRIS COLE, born March 10, 1982, in Statesville, North Carolina. Cole is big by street skating standards. At 6' 1" and 190 pounds, he can consistently land tough tricks and make them look easy. A newcomer to the contest scene, he won a gold medal at the Gravity Games and a bronze in Street at the X Games in 2005.

10 LYN-Z ADAMS HAWKINS, born September 21, 1989, in Cardiff-by-the-Sea, California. This 16-year-old oozes potential and is on track to take women's riding to the next level. She can ride any terrain. At age 14, she won X Games gold in women's Vert by becoming the first woman to land a kickflip indy.

Lyn-Z Adams Hawkins

X GAMES RESULTS

MEN

YEAR	EVENT	GOLD	SILVER	BRONZE
2003	Park	Ryan Sheckler, U.S.	Rodil de Araujo, Jr., Brazil	Chad Bartie, Australia
2002	Park	Rodil de Araujo, Jr., Brazil	Wagner Ramos, Brazil	Eric Koston, U.S.
2001	Park	Rodil de Araujo, Jr., Brazil	Kerry Getz, U.S.	Caine Gayle, U.S.
2000	Park	Eric Koston, U.S.	Rodil de Araujo, Jr., Brazil	Kerry Getz, U.S.
2005	Street	Paul Rodriguez, U.S.	Greg Lutzka, U.S.	Chris Cole, U.S.
2004	Street	Paul Rodriguez, U.S.	Andrew Reynolds, U.S.	Bastien Salabanzi, France
2003	Street	Eric Koston, U.S.	Rodil de Araujo, Jr., Brazil	Paul Rodriguez, U.S.
2002	Street	Rodil de Araujo, Jr., Brazil	Wagner Ramos, Brazil	Kyle Berard, U.S.
2001	Street	Kerry Getz, U.S.	Eric Koston, U.S.	Chris Senn, U.S.
1999	Street	Chris Senn, U.S.	Pat Channita, U.S.	Chad Fernandez, U.S.
1998	Street	Rodil de Araujo, Jr., Brazil	Andy Macdonald, U.S.	Chris Senn, U.S.
1997	Street	Chris Senn, U.S.	Andy Macdonald, U.S.	Brian Patch, U.S.
1996	Street	Rodil de Araujo, Jr., Brazil	Chris Senn, U.S.	Brian Patch, U.S.
1995	Street	Chris Senn, U.S.	Tony Hawk, U.S.	Willy Santos, U.S.
2003	Street Best Trick	Chad Muska, U.S.	Rodil de Araujo, Jr., Brazil	Wagner Ramos, Brazil
2002	Street Best Trick	Rodil de Araujo, Jr., Brazil	Wagner Ramos, Brazil	Dayne Brummet, U.S.
2001	Street Best Trick	Rick McCrank, Canada	Kerry Getz, U.S.	Eric Koston, U.S.
1996	Street Best Trick	Gershon Mosley, U.S.	Chris Senn, U.S.	Brian Patch, U.S.
1995	Street Best Trick	Jamie Thomas, U.S.	Gershon Mosley, U.S.	Kareem Campbell, U.S.
2005	Vert	Pierre-Luc Gagnon, Canada	Shaun White, U.S.	Sandro Dias, Brazil
2004	Vert	Bucky Lasek, U.S.	Pierre-Luc Gagnon, Canada	Rune Glifberg, Denmark
2003	Vert	Bucky Lasek, U.S.	Andy Macdonald, U.S.	Rune Glifberg, Denmark
2002	Vert	Pierre-Luc Gagnon, Canada	Bob Burnquist, Brazil	Rune Glifberg, Denmark
2001	Vert	Bob Burnquist, Brazil	Bucky Lasek, U.S.	Tas Pappas, Australia
2000	Vert	Bucky Lasek, U.S.	Pierre-Luc Gagnon, Canada	Colin McKay, Canada
1999	Vert	Bucky Lasek, U.S.	Andy Macdonald, U.S.	Tony Hawk, U.S.
1998	Vert	Andy Macdonald, U.S.	Giorgio Zattoni, Italy	Tony Hawk, U.S.
1997	Vert	Tony Hawk, U.S.	Rune Glifberg, Denmark	Bob Burnquist, Brazil
1996	Vert	Andy Macdonald, U.S.	Tony Hawk, U.S.	Tas Pappas, Australia
1995	Vert	Tony Hawk, U.S.	Neal Hendrix, U.S.	Rune Glifberg, Denmark
2005	Vert Best Trick	Bob Burnquist, Brazil	Colin McKay, Canada	Pierre-Luc Gagnon, Canada
2004	Vert Best Trick	Sandro Dias, Brazil	Pierre-Luc Gagnon, Canada	Danny Mayer, U.S.
2003	Vert Best Trick	Tony Hawk, U.S.	Sandro Dias, Brazil	Andy Macdonald, U.S.
2002	Vert Best Trick	Pierre-Luc Gagnon, Canada	Sandro Dias, Brazil	Tony Hawk, U.S.
2001	Vert Best Trick	Matt Dove, U.S.	Tony Hawk, U.S.	Bob Burnquist, Brazil
2000	Vert Best Trick	Bob Burnquist, Brazil	Colin McKay, Canada	Andy Macdonald, U.S.
1999	Vert Best Trick	Tony Hawk, U.S.	Colin McKay, Canada	Bob Burnquist, Brazil
2005	Big Air	Danny Way, U.S.	Pierre-Luc Gagnon, Canada	Andy Macdonald, U.S.
2004	Big Air	Danny Way, U.S.	Pierre-Luc Gagnon, Canada	Andy Macdonald, U.S.
2003	Vert Doubles	Bucky Lasek, U.S. / Bob Burnquist, Brazil	Rune Glifberg, Denmark / Mike Crum, U.S.	Neal Hendrix, U.S. / Buster Halterman, U.S.
2002	Vert Doubles	Tony Hawk, U.S. / Andy Macdonald, U.S.	Bucky Lasek, U.S. / Bob Burnquist, Brazil	Rune Glifberg, Denmark. / Mike Crum, U.S.
2001	Vert Doubles	Tony Hawk, U.S. / Andy Macdonald, U.S.	Mike Crum, U.S. / Chris Gentry, U.S.	Mike Frazier, U.S. / Neal Hendrix, U.S.
2000	Vert Doubles	Tony Hawk, U.S. / Andy Macdonald, U.S.	Pierre-Luc Gagnon, Canada / Max Dufour, Canada	Sandro Dias, Brazil / Cristiano Mateus, Brazil
1999	Vert Doubles	Tony Hawk, U.S. / Andy Macdonald, U.S.	Bucky Lasek, U.S. / Brian Patch, U.S.	Rune Glifberg, Denmark / Mike Crum, U.S.
1998	Vert Doubles	Tony Hawk, U.S. / Andy Macdonald, U.S.	Bucky Lasek, U.S. / Brian Patch, U.S.	Bob Burnquist, Brazil / Lincoln Ueda, Brazil
1997	Vert Doubles	Tony Hawk, U.S. / Andy Macdonald, U.S.	Mike Frazier, U.S. / Neal Hendrix, U.S.	Max Dufour, Canada / Mathias Ringstrom, Sweden
1995	High Air	Danny Way, U.S.	Neal Hendrix, U.S.	Tas Pappas, Australia

X GAMES RESULTS (CONT.)

WOMEN

YEAR	EVENT	GOLD	SILVER	BRONZE
2005	Street	Elissa Steamer, U.S.	Evelien Bouilliart, Belgium	Marissa Del Santo, U.S.
2004	Street	Elissa Steamer, U.S.	Vanessa Torres, U.S.	Lauren Perkins, U.S.
2005	Vert	Cara-Beth Burnside, U.S.	Lyn-Z Adams Hawkins, U.S.	Mimi Knoop, U.S.
2004	Vert	Lyn-Z Adams Hawkins, U.S.	Cara-Beth Burnside, U.S.	Mimi Knoop, U.S.

GRAVITY GAMES RESULTS

MEN

YEAR	EVENT	GOLD	SILVER	BRONZE
2005	Vert	Bucky Lasek, U.S.	Andy Macdonald, U.S.	Sandro Dias, Brazil
2004	Vert	Rune Glifberg, Denmark	Andy Macdonald, U.S.	Pierre-Luc Gagnon, Canada
2003	Vert	Bucky Lasek, U.S.	Andy Macdonald, U.S.	Rune Glifberg, Denmark
2002	Vert	Bucky Lasek, U.S.	Bob Burnquist, Brazil	Pierre-Luc Gagnon, Canada
2001	Vert	Rune Glifberg, Denmark	Bucky Lasek, U.S.	Andy Macdonald, U.S.
2000	Vert	Andy Macdonald, U.S.	Bob Burnquist, Brazil	Pierre-Luc Gagnon, Canada
1999	Vert	Bob Burnquist, Brazil	Bucky Lasek, U.S.	Andy Macdonald, U.S.
2005	Vert Best Trick	Bucky Lasek, U.S.	Pierre-Luc Gagnon, Canada	Sandro Dias, Brazil
2004	Vert Best Trick	Sandro Dias, Brazil	Danny Mayer, U.S.	Pierre-Luc Gagnon, Canada
2003	Vert Best Trick	Mathias Ringstrom, Sweden	Danny Mayer, U.S.	Sandro Diaz, Brazil
2002	Vert Best Trick	Pierre-Luc Gagnon, Canada	Bob Burnquist, Brazil	Sandro Diaz, Brazil
2005	Street	Chris Cole, U.S.	Wagner Ramos, Brazil	Andre Genovesi, Brazil
2004	Street	Rodil de Araujo, Jr., Brazil	Greg Lutzka, U.S.	Ryan Sheckler, U.S.
2003	Street	Ryan Sheckler, U.S.	Rick McCrank, Canada	Chris Senn, U.S.
2002	Street	Eric Koston, U.S.	Pat Channita, U.S.	Kerry Getz, U.S.
2001	Street	Eric Koston, U.S.	Rick McCrank, Canada	Kyle Berard, U.S.
2000	Street	Eric Koston, U.S.	Brian Anderson, U.S.	Kerry Getz, U.S.
1999	Street	Brian Anderson, U.S.	Rodil de Araujo, Jr., Brazil	Eric Koston, U.S.
2005	Street Best Trick	Andre Genovesi, Brazil	Not awarded	Not awarded
2004	Street Best Trick	Paul Machnau, Canada	Nilton Neves, Brazil	Josh Evin, Canada
2003	Street Best Trick	Chris Haslam, Canada	Daniel Vieira, Brazil	Chad Bartie, Australia
2005	Park	Omar Hassan, U.S.	Kyle Berard, U.S.	Benji Galloway, U.S.
2002	Downhill, 2-person	Mark Golter, U.S.	Dane Van Bommel, U.S.	Alex Wenk, Switzerland
2001	Downhill, 2-person	Dane Van Bommel, U.S.	Gary Hardwick, U.S.	Mark Golter, U.S.
2000	Downhill, 2-person	Dane Van Bommel, U.S.	John Gwiazdowski, U.S.	Alex Wenk, Switzerland
1999	Downhill, 2-person	Lee Dansie, Great Britain	Biker Sherlock, U.S.	Dane Van Bommel, U.S.
2002	Downhill, 4-person	Darryl Freeman, U.S.	Mark Golter, U.S.	Dane Van Bommel, U.S.
2001	Downhill, 4-person	Dane Van Bommel, U.S.	Alex Wenk, Switzerland	Lee Dansie, Great Britain
2000	Downhill, 4-person	Dane Van Bommel, U.S.	John Gwiazdowski, U.S.	Alex Wenk, Switzerland
1999	Downhill, 4-person	Biker Sherlock, U.S.	Dane Van Bommel, U.S.	Emanuel Antuna, France

WOMEN

YEAR	EVENT	GOLD	SILVER	BRONZE
2005	Street	Not held	Not held	Not held
2004	Street	Elissa Steamer, U.S.	Lauren Perkins, U.S.	Lyn-Z Adams Hawkins, U.S.

MONSTER MASTERSHIP RESULTS

MEN

YEAR	EVENT	GOLD	SILVER	BRONZE
2005	Street	Daniel Vieira, Brazil	Ricardo Oliveira Porva, Brazil	Ryan Sheckler, U.S.
2004	Street	Bastien Salabanzi, France	Daniel Vieira, Brazil	Rodil de Araujo, Jr., Brazil
2003	Street	Greg Lutzka, U.S.	Allan Mesquita, Brazil	Colt Cannon, U.S.
2002	Street	Bastien Salabanzi, France	Chris Senn, U.S.	Rodil de Araujo, Jr., Brazil
2001	Street	Bastien Salabanzi, France	Rodil de Araujo, Jr., Brazil	Rick McCrank, Canada
2000	Street	Eric Koston, U.S.	Ryan Johnson, Puerto Rico	Rick McCrank, Canada
1999	Street	Brian Anderson, U.S.	Rick McCrank, Canada	Andrew Reynolds, U.S.
1998	Street	Brian Anderson, U.S.	Arto Saari, Finland	Chris Senn, U.S.
1997	Street	Willy Santos, U.S.	Chris Senn, U.S.	Donny Barley, U.S.
1996	Street	Ruben Raibal, Germany	Fabio Fusco, Germany	Tim Liebthal, Spain
1995	Street	Chris Senn, U.S.	Ed Templeton, U.S.	Mako Urabe, U.S.
1994	Street	Ethan Fowler, U.S.	Wade Speyer, U.S.	Ed Templeton, U.S.
1993	Street	Ed Templeton, U.S.	Tony Hawk, U.S.	Pat Duffy, U.S.
1992	Street	Sami Harithi, Germany	Mike Manzoori, Great Britain	Dirk Winkelman, New Zealand
1991	Street	Tony Hawk, U.S.	Alan Peterson, U.S.	Jason Rogers, U.S.
1990	Street	Ed Templeton, U.S	Eric Dressen, U.S.	Danny Way, U.S.
1989	Street	Lance Mountain, U.S.	Tony Hawk, U.S.	Ray Barbee, U.S.
1988	Street	Steve Caballero, U.S.	Christian Hosoi, U.S.	Tommy Guerrero, U.S.
1987	Street	Steve Caballero, U.S.	Lance Mountain, U.S.	Nicky Guerrero, Denmark
2005	Vert	Sandro Dias, Brazil	Mathias Ringstrom, Sweden	Cristiano Mateus, Brazil
2004	Vert	Andy Macdonald, U.S.	Mike Crum, U.S.	Neal Hendrix, U.S.
2003	Vert	Pierre-Luc Gagnon, Canada	Rune Glifberg, Denmark	Andy Macdonald, U.S.
2002	Vert	Pierre-Luc Gagnon, Canada	Rune Glifberg, Denmark	Andy Macdonald, U.S.
2001	Vert	Rune Glifberg, Denmark	Sandro Dias, Brazil	Matt Dove, U.S.
2000	Vert	Bob Burnquist, Brazil	Pierre-Luc Gagnon, Canada	Rune Glifberg, Denmark
1999	Vert	Bucky Lasek, U.S.	Tas Pappas, Australia	Andy Macdonald, U.S.
1998	Vert	Tony Hawk, U.S.	Bob Burnquist, Brazil	Mathias Ringstrom, Sweden
1997	Vert	Andy Macdonald, U.S.	Bob Burnquist, Brazil	Chris Gentry, U.S.
1996	Vert	Oli Burgin, Switzerland	Fabio Fusco, Germany	Bernt Jahnel, Germany
1995	Vert	Rodrigo Menezes, Brazil	Colin McKay, Canada	Mike Frazier, U.S.
1994	Vert	Mike Frazier, U.S.	Neal Hendrix, U.S.	Andy Macdonald, U.S.
1993	Vert	Tony Hawk, U.S.	Mike Frazier, U.S.	Rune Glifberg, Denmark
1992	Vert	Rune Glifberg, Denmark	Bod Boyle, Great Britain	Paul Robson, Great Britain
1991	Vert	Tony Hawk, U.S.	Chris Miller, U.S.	Steve Caballero, U.S.
1990	Vert	Bod Boyle, U.S.	Chris Miller, U.S.	Danny Way, U.S.
1989	Vert	Tony Hawk, U.S.	Tony Magnusson, U.S.	Jeff Kendall, U.S.
1988	Vert	Christian Hosoi, U.S.	Steve Caballero, U.S.	Jason Jessee, U.S.
1987	Vert	Steve Caballero, U.S.	Lance Mountain, U.S.	Nicky Guerrero, Denmark
1992	Freestyle	Gunter Mokulys, Germany	Jorg Finger, Germany	Christian Seewaldt, Germany
1991	Freestyle	Gunter Mokulys, Germany	Don Brown, Great Britain	Jean Marc Vaissette, France
1990	Freestyle	Rodney Mullen, U.S.	Pierre Andre Senizergues, France	Don Brown, U.S.
1989	Freestyle	Don Brown, U.S.	Pierre Andre Senizergues, France	Gunter Mokulys, Germany
1988	Freestyle	Pierre Andre Senizergues, France	Jean Marc Vaissette, France	Don Brown, Great Britain
1987	Freestyle	Jean Marc Vaissette, France	Shane Rouse, Great Britain	Reggie Barnes, U.S.

WOMEN

YEAR	EVENT	GOLD	SILVER	BRONZE
2005	Street	Elissa Steamer, U.S.	Vanessa Torres, U.S	Evelien Bouilliart, Belgium
2004	Street	Vanessa Torres, U.S.	Lauren Perkins, U.S.	Lyn-Z Adams Hawkins, U.S.
2005	Vert	Karen Jones, Brazil	Tina Neff, Germany	Rebecca Aimee Davies, England

DEW ACTION SPORTS TOUR CHAMPIONS

YEAR	EVENT	
2005	Street	Ryan Sheckler, U.S.
2005	Vert	Bucky Lasek, U.S.

SLAM CITY JAM RESULTS

MEN

YEAR	EVENT	GOLD	SILVER	BRONZE
2005	Street	Paul Rodriguez, U.S.	Jereme Rogers, U.S.	Ryan Sheckler, U.S.
2004	Street	Greg Lutzka, U.S.	Rodil de Araujo, Jr., Brazil	Ryan Sheckler, U.S.
2003	Street	Ryan Sheckler, U.S.	Rick McCrank, Canada	Carlos de Andrade, Brazil
2002	Street	Rodil de Araujo, Jr., Brazil	Eric Koston, U.S.	Paul Rodriguez, U.S.
2001	Street	Eric Koston, U.S.	Colt Cannon, U.S.	Rick McCrank, Canada
2005	Vert	Pierre-Luc Gagnon, Canada	Bob Burnquist, Brazil	Bucky Lasek, U.S.
2004	Vert	Bucky Lasek, U.S.	Chris Gentry, U.S.	Sandro Dias, Brazil
2003	Vert	Sandro Dias, Brazil	Andy Macdonald, U.S.	Jake Brown, U.S.
2002	Vert	Buckey Lasek, U.S.	Pierre-Luc Gagnon, Canada	Sandro Dias, Brazil
2001	Vert	Bob Burnquist, Brazil	Rune Glifberg, Denmark	Bucky Lasek, U.S.

WOMEN

YEAR	EVENT	GOLD	SILVER	BRONZE
2005	Street	Amy Caron, U.S.	Lacey Baker, U.S.	Lauren Perkins, U.S.
2004	Street	Vanessa Torres, U.S.	Elissa Steamer, U.S.	Lauren Perkins, U.S.
2003	Street	Vanessa Torres, U.S.	Lauren Perkins, U.S.	Monica Shaw, Australia
2002	Street	Amy Caron, U.S.	Vanessa Torres, U.S.	Lauren Perkins, U.S.
2005	Vert	Cara-Beth Burnside, U.S.	Mimi Knoop, U.S.	Lyn-Z Adams Hawkins, U.S.
2004	Vert	Cara-Beth Burnside, U.S.	Mimi Knoop, U.S.	Lyn-Z Adams Hawkins, U.S.
2003	Vert	Cara-Beth Burnside, U.S.	Jen O'Brien, U.S.	Lyn-Z Adams Hawkins, U.S.
2002	Vert	Jen O'Brien, U.S.	Jessica Starkweather, U.S.	Heidi Fitzgerald, U.S.
2001	Vert	Jen O'Brien, U.S.	Candy Hiler, U.S.	Jodie MacDonald, U.S.

GLOBE WORLD CUP RESULTS

YEAR	EVENT	
2005	Overall	Bastien Salabanzi, France
2004	Overall	Ronnie Creager, U.S.
2003	Street	Carlos de Andrade, Brazil
2002	Street	Rick McCrank, Canada
2003	Vert	Sandro Dias, Brazil
2002	Vert	Bucky Lasek, U.S.

GALLAZ SKATE JAM RESULTS

YEAR	
2005	Elissa Steamer, U.S.
2004	Elissa Steamer, U.S.
2003	Not held
2002	Amy Caron, U.S.

TOP 10 PLACES TO RIDE

1 CAMP WOODWARD, PENNSYLVANIA; LAKE OWEN, WISCONSIN; WOODWARD WEST, CALIFORNIA. These camps are the ultimate in terrain and training facilities. They are sleepaway camps during the summer, but top pros visit year-round to train in their innovative foam pits and on their resi (soft) ramps. The high-tech facilities allow skaters to learn tricks without risking serious injury. With dozens of indoor and outdoor street courses, vert ramps, and bowls, the Woodward camps are a skater's paradise.

Los Angeles, California

2 LOS ANGELES, CALIFORNIA, STREETS. There are so many hot skating spots in the greater Los Angeles area that it would be impossible to list them all. Open any skateboard magazine or pop in a video and chances are that most of the images were shot somewhere in L.A. Some highlights: Whittier High School's 10-stair ledge and 7-stair rail; the Santa Monica courthouse's stage, planters, handrails, and stairs; and Los Angeles High School's ledges, stairs, banks, and rails.

Magdalena Ecke Family YMCA Skatepark

3 MAGDALENA ECKE FAMILY YMCA SKATEPARK, ENCINITAS, CALIFORNIA. This is a favorite park for many of the top pros in the San Diego area, including Andy Macdonald, Shaun White, Tony Hawk, and Lyn-Z Adams Hawkins. The park has just about everything, including a challenging street section, concrete pools, and a 13-foot-tall, 160-foot-long halfpipe. The park is open to the public, so anyone can watch or skate with the world's best.

4 SAN FRANCISCO, CALIFORNIA, STREETS. During the 1980's, Mark Gonzales and Tommy Guerrero practically invented modern street skating at San Francisco's many legendary spots. One of the best, The Embarcadero, has been renovated as a shopping area and is now less skateable. But other areas, such as Pier 7 (stairs) and Third and Army (ledges and a gap), still rule. Want to learn to ride handrails? Go to school: The handrails outside Jefferson Elementary and Wallenberg Traditional High School have been featured in dozens of skate videos.

5 FDR SKATEPARK, PHILADELPHIA, PENNSYLVANIA. This public park was built in 1994 after skaters were kicked out of Love Park, a stellar street spot in the city center. Skaters found the terrain lacking, so they began adding on to it themselves. The result: a masterpiece of concrete bowls, bunkers, moguls, and banks. FDR is a gritty spot located underneath the interstate and completely covered in graffiti.

FDR Skatepark

6 BARCELONA, SPAIN, STREETS. Barcelona is a favorite destination of skaters due to its pleasant weather and miles of skateable urban terrain. The public squares and marble steps of the city's many churches are fair game for skaters. But the best spots are the ledges and benches at the Museum of Contemporary Art and the Port Olympic skatepark right next to the beach.

Barcelona, Spain

HELGE TSCHARN/RED BULL

7 MISSION VALLEY YMCA: KRAUSE FAMILY SKATEPARK, SAN DIEGO, CALIFORNIA. While not as impressive as its counterpart in Encinitas, Mission Valley still offers a deep concrete pool, a street course, a slew of mini-ramps, and a huge halfpipe. Many top pros ride here (Andy Macdonald even helped design it), but terrain for beginners makes it appealing to all levels.

Marseille Skatepark

8 BROOKLYN BANKS, NEW YORK CITY. The Banks is located at the base of the Brooklyn Bridge on the Manhattan side. It has been a legendary spot for more than 20 years. It is part of a public park and is a series of brick-paved banks with ledges, rails, and walls.

9 MARSEILLE SKATEPARK, MARSEILLE, FRANCE. Marseille Skatepark was built in 1991. It is one of the world's most famous concrete parks and attracts many top pros. The park offers something for everyone. It maintains a strong family vibe, with kids and their parents often skating together.

10 SKATEPARK OF TAMPA (SPOT), TAMPA, FLORIDA. This park is home to the annual Tampa Pro contest in March. It features indoor street and bowls and outdoor vert ramps, all of which are updated each year. SPOT has a great reputation among pros for supporting skateboarding through the lean times of the early 1990's.

Skatepark of Tampa

SKATEPARK OF TAMPA

CHAPTER 5

SKIING

As if speeding down a mountain isn't exciting enough, skiers continue to find ways to make their sport even more extreme.

Tanner Hall is the king of park, pipe, and back-country freeskiing.

CHRIS O'CONNELL

Skiing is one of our oldest sports: It dates back almost 5,000 years. Archaeologists have found rock paintings in Europe, near the Arctic Circle, that show hunters and trappers chasing their prey on skis.

The sport began as a means of transportation during the long, snowy winters in the Scandinavian countries of northern Europe (today's Denmark, Finland, Iceland, Norway, and Sweden). By the mid-1800's, changes in lifestyle as well as improvements in equipment and technique led to the growth of recreational skiing, which evolved into the sport we know today.

The Man Who Changed Everything

There were skiing competitions in Scandinavia as early as the late 1700's. People participated in what we now call Nordic skiing, a type of skiing that included cross-country, uphill, some downhill, and ski jumping. Skiers made their own skis or had a local craftsman make them a pair. They attached their boots to their skis.

Sondre Norheim, a potato farmer from the Telemark region of Norway, introduced modern skiing in the late 1800's. Norheim, who was also a competitive skier, invented new techniques and equipment that allowed people to ski better.

Norheim pioneered a new style of turning called Telemark (after his home region) that gave skiers more control on a downhill run. In a Telemark turn, the skier would bend his knee and raise his heel to pivot the inside ski while keeping most of his weight on the downhill ski. Norheim invented Telemark bindings, which attached the boot to the ski at the toe, allowing the heel to rise up.

He also created a heel strap that was flexible but secure. It allowed skiers to turn harder and soar off jumps without losing their skis. Norheim improved his skis, too. He made them narrower near the middle, which made them more flexible and better in soft snow.

Using superior technique and equipment, Norheim dominated both Slalom and Ski Jumping competitions. Soon, others began copying Norheim's Telemark style of skiing as well as his skis.

Sarah Burke is a force in women's Superpipe.

By 1900, skiing had spread around the world, but was especially popular in the Alps mountain range in Europe. The Alps run through 11 countries, including Austria, Italy, France, and Switzerland.

Taking It Down the Mountain

Skiers in the Alps began to interpret the sport in their own way. Instead of skiing cross-country, they raced downhill. Their approach would be called Alpine skiing, named after the mountain range in which it developed.

One of the early Alpine skiers, Johannes Schneider of the Arlsberg region of Austria, developed a way of teaching downhill skiing that helped bring the sport to the world.

Schneider had been Austria's national ski champion. During World War I, he taught members of the Austrian army to ski. He instructed hundreds of students at a time, and developed a teaching method he would use later in his ski school back in Arlberg. The Arlberg System worked so well that it is still the basis for ski instruction today.

Alpine skiing received another "lift" in the 1920's, when ski lifts were invented in Europe. People no longer had to hike up a mountain before they could ski down it.

No trick is too big for C.R. Johnson.

CHRIS O'CONNELL

10th Mountain Division returned to the U.S. and started skiing businesses.

Technological advances during the war also led to better equipment. Previously, skis and poles were made from wood, which broke easily. Boots were made from leather, which got wet and stretched. Bindings were difficult to fasten and would remain locked even during a bad wipeout.

Some of the innovations in equipment included step-in bindings that released during wipeouts; aluminum, and then fiberglass, skis; plastic-molded buckle boots; and aluminum poles. Another major invention that boosted skiing — especially on the East Coast, where snow could be inconsistent — was the snowmaking machine.

By 1960, the first Winter Olympics featuring Alpine events was held in the U.S., at Squaw Valley, California. Jean Vuarnet of France became the first skier to compete on metal skis and won the gold medal in the Downhill event.

Instead, they rode the lift up the mountain, raced down, then rode up again.

In competitions, Alpine events, such as Downhill and Slalom racing, were gaining popularity. The first-known Alpine race was held in 1911 in Montana, Switzerland. The first Slalom race was held in 1922 in Mürren, Switzerland. In Downhill, skiers race to be the fastest to get to the bottom of the course. In Slalom, skiers must zigzag across the mountain, passing around gates or flags.

Still, Alpine was slow to gain acceptance where it counted most — with the sport's international sanctioning body, the Fédération Internationale de Ski (FIS). Most FIS officials were Nordic skiers. They didn't sanction the first Alpine world championship until 1931. Alpine events didn't make their Olympic debut until the 1936 Games in Garmisch-Partenkirchen, Germany.

During the 1930's, Alpine skiing spread to North America. Several Austrian ski instructors, including Johannes Schneider, fled their country to escape the Nazis and came to the United States. Alpine skiing got another boost in 1936, when the ski resort at Sun Valley, Idaho, introduced the first chairlift.

New Materials, Better Equipment

Most ski resorts were closed during World War II. After the war, many trained skiers who had served in the Army's

The Freestyle Revolution

Downhill, Slalom, and Giant Slalom were the official Alpine events in the 1960's. By 1967, FIS had adopted an annual men's and women's Alpine World Cup series. Skiers competed to accumulate the most combined points during a season of those events.

However, away from the competitions, another form of skiing was becoming popular. In the 1960's, skiers in the U.S. began to explore freestyle skiing, a more creative form of the sport that had long been big in Europe. It went by different names: hotdogging, freeskiing, and freestyle.

Stein Eriksen was responsible for popularizing freestyle in the U.S. He had emigrated from Norway after winning the gold medal in Giant Slalom and the silver in Slalom at the 1952 Winter Olympics. Eriksen developed his own style of turning and jumping, even doing flips. As he traveled around the U.S., other skiers copied his moves.

FAST FACT

Jean-Claude Killy of France was the last skier to sweep the Alpine events at the Olympics. He won gold medals in Downhill, Slalom, and Giant Slalom at the 1968 Games. (Super Giant Slalom, or Super G, was added in 1988.)

Just as with Alpine skiing, the FIS was slow to accept [fre]estyle. But the new type of skiing kept growing. After a [fail]ed pro tour in the mid-1970's, the World Cup freestyle [ser]ies debuted in 1980, featuring Moguls, Aerials, and [Bal]let events.

[Ski]ing to the Extreme

[Sk]iers looking for even more thrills moved on to [ext]reme skiing, a noncompetitive form of the sport where [the]y charged over backcountry terrain full of deep [po]wder and sheer cliffs. Here, even a small slipup could [me]an death. By the late 1980's, ski films and videos had [ma]de stars of early extreme skiers such as Glen Plake [an]d Scott Schmidt.

Freestyle was booming. The term "freeskiing" came to [be] used to cover all the new forms of skiing outside of [Alp]ine and Nordic — extreme, freestyle, and jibbing. [Mo]guls skiing, in which skiers race down a bumpy run [an]d pull tricks, was added to the Olympics in 1992. Two years later, Aerials, where skiers launch high and spin and flip for judged scores, joined the Olympics, too.

In spite of all this, skiing began to lose participants to the new sport of snowboarding. Snowboarding seemed cooler and more fun. It was time to take freeskiing to another level.

At the 1998 Winter Olympics, Jonny Moseley, a moguls skier from California, borrowed a move from snowboarding, hucked a stylish 360 mute grab, and won the gold medal. Meanwhile, other young skiers were imitating boarders' gnarly moves in halfpipes, and a jibbing movement (skiing on rails, ledges, and obstacles) took hold in terrain parks. The Winter X Games added skiing Superpipe and Slopestyle events in 2002. Tanner Hall emerged as the dominant athlete in both, winning four gold and three silver medals.

For freeskiers today, it's all about creativity. Just as it's been ever since those early Nordic skiers, the only limits are their imagination and ability.

[I]NNOVATOR
GLEN PLAKE

Glen Plake is famous for his foot-high multi-colored Mohawk hairstyle. But he has earned the respect of skiers everywhere for his hair-raising stunts. Plake grew up skiing at Heavenly Mountain Resort in Lake Tahoe, California, during the 1970's. He was a member of the resort's racing team. At the time, Heavenly was home to some of the world's best freeskiers — people who leaped off cliffs, made jumps, and bounded over moguls. Inspired, Plake began imitating them, booming down the resort's icy mogul run and launching into the air. He became so good that by 1985 he was invited to join the U.S. Ski Team. But no coaches could tame him or his skiing. Plake returned to freeskiing full-time, and eventually found another way to make his mark in the sport. In 1988, he starred in the ski film, *Blizzard of Aahhh's*, which introduced the world to freeskiing. In one segment, Plake hucked himself off a cliff in the Alps near Chamonix, France, and wiped out, cartwheeling down the steep face. Viewers were in awe of his skill and daring. Plake inspired others to follow in his tracks, including today's hard-core risk-takers Seth Morrison and Shane McConkey. Before Plake, skiing's stars mostly came from Alpine racing. But Plake showed that the path to stardom sometimes leads over cliffs and through deep powder.

SCOTT MARKEWITZ

GROUNDBREAKING TRICK
DINNER ROLL

JONNY MOSELEY

Jonny Moseley had brought a new degree of difficulty to freestyle skiing at the 1998 Winter Olympics. He won the gold medal in Moguls with a new-school trick, a 360 mute grab. But for the 2002 Games, Moseley planned a bigger trick: the dinner roll (with his body parallel to the ground, Moseley would spin a barrel roll for two rotations). However, such tricks were banned from the Olympics because they were done off-axis (with the skis either level with or over the skier's head). After much convincing, Moseley was permitted to do his trick at the Games. In the finals, he stuck a couple of flawless dinner rolls, and the crowd went nuts. The judges weren't as impressed, and Moseley finished fourth. Still, Moseley had put a new style of trick on the freestyle menu.

DOUGLAS C. PIZAC/AP

TIME LINE

2,500 B.C.
Rock paintings and skis preserved in bogs show that hunters and trappers in northern Europe used skis almost 5,000 years ago.

1866 Sondre Norheim
demonstrates the Telemark turn and skidding stop in an exhibition in Norway, changing skiing technique forever.

Sondre Norheim

COURTESY OF THE U.S. NATIONAL SKI HALL OF FAME AND MUSEUM

1882 The first
ski club in the United States is founded in Berlin, New Hampshire.

1918 Johannes Schneider of
Arlberg, Austria, starts a ski school. His teaching method becomes the foundation for ski lessons today.

82 SKIING

NECESSARY
OBJECTS

- **SKIS:** All skis have the same basic design: tip, tail, metal edges, sidecut, topskin, and base. There are many options, but unless you're an expert, you'll only need to focus on a few things when choosing the skis that are right for you.

  Sidecut radius is an important consideration. Measured in meters (m), sidecut determines how narrow the ski is toward the middle. The greater the sidecut, the easier the ski will turn. Most skis have a sidecut radius of around 25 m.

  Also important is ski length, measured in centimeters (cm). Skis range in length from 120 cm to 220 cm. Beginners should use shorter skis, which sacrifice speed for control. A good rule of thumb: If you stand your skis on end, the tips should reach to between your shoulders and eyebrows.

- **BINDINGS:** Bindings attach the skis to the boot. They are simply stepped into, clicking a heelpiece into place. To release the boots from the bindings, just push down on a lever on the heelpiece and step out. Bindings also automatically release from the boots during wipeouts, when skis can twist legs into awkward and painful positions. Brakes are another safety feature found on bindings: Two prongs spring downward when the bindings release, digging into the snow and preventing loose skis from rocketing down the slope and striking others.

- **BOOTS:** You should own your boots even if you rent everything else. Boots are your connection to the skis and should fit comfortably. Ski boots have hard molded-plastic shells with toe- and heelpieces that fit into any bindings. Buckles fasten them tight. Inside the hard shell is a soft foam liner.

- **POLES:** Poles help with balance and turning. You can tell if a pole is your size by holding it upside down with the grip touching the floor. Grab it just under the basket (the circular piece near the tip). If your arm is parallel to the floor, then the pole is the right size.

- **HELMET:** Helmets are always a good idea, especially if you're going to be trying tricks. Make sure a helmet is CEN rated (Central European standard) for safety and fits properly, especially with your goggles on.

- **GOGGLES:** Goggles protect eyes from snow, wind, sun, and branches. Better ones have UV protection and act like sunglasses, which helps on bright days when snow causes glare.

924 **The first Olympic** ter Games are held at monix, France. Only dic skiing events, such ross-Country and Ski ping, are included.

1930 **Rudolph Lettner,** a metal worker from Salzburg, Austria, invents a steel edge that prevent skis from wearing down. The edges also improve turning on hard snow.

1932 **The Winter** Olympics are held in the U.S. for the first time. Downhill and Slalom skiing events are still excluded.

COURTESY OF THE COMMUNITY LIBRARY/REGIONAL HISTORY DEPT.

Sun Valley

1936 **The Sun** Valley resort opens in Idaho, featuring the world's first chairlift.

THE BASIC TRICKS

DAFFY▶

To do a daffy, you must be comfortable in the air. Once you have liftoff, extend one leg in front of you and the other in back. If done properly, the front ski points upward and the rear ski downward, as if you were frozen in the middle of a running motion. From there, progress to a double daffy, and switch your legs in midair before landing.

GEORGE FREY/AP

◀ BACK-SCRATCHER

Try this once you're comfortable with a daffy. In a backscratcher, you extend both skis behind your body, pointing downward. The skis' tails should reach almost high enough to scratch your back. Then, get your skis back under you. Catching your tips in the snow will lead to a face plant.

DOUGLAS C. PIZAC/AP

HELICOPTER▶

More of an intermediate move, a helicopter is simply a spin off a jump. Once you're in the air, turn your head and shoulders right or left (whichever direction is more comfortable). Your body and skis will follow naturally without too much effort. Spin one full rotation and then spot your landing before stomping down with your skis. Once you're comfortable with helicopters, progress to 720s (two full rotations).

BRIAN BAHR/GETTY IMAGES

TIME LINE

1948 Gretchen Fraser becomes the first American to win Olympic ski medals — gold in Slalom and silver in Alpine Combined.

1959 The first fiberglass ski is invented in Montreal, Canada.

Jean-Claude Killy

AP

1968 French racer Jean-Claude Killy sweeps all three Alpine events at the Winter Olympics in Grenoble, France, winning Downhill, Slalom, and Giant Slalom.

< L E G E N D >
JONNY MOSELEY

By the late 1990's, snowboarding had elbowed its way on to the slopes. Not only did skiers have to share the mountain, they suddenly seemed a lot less cool. Snowboarding was hip, while skiing was for geezers. Even in freestyle competitions, judges seldom rewarded creativity. As a result, many skiers seldom tried anything new. The sport was, in the words of freestyle moguls skier Jonny Moseley, "in need of a 'hip' replacement."

Moseley had been a ski prodigy as a teen in California. At 15, he won the 1990 Junior National Freestyle Championship. When he failed to qualify for the 1994 Winter Olympics, Moseley began working on a trick inspired by snowboarding — the 360 mute grab (a spin where he crossed his skis behind his back and grabbed his left ski).

In Moguls, competitors race down a course and pull tricks while soaring off icy bumps. Scores are based on speed, style, and trick difficulty. At the 1998 Winter Olympics, Moseley's 360 mute grab wowed the crowd and judges. He won the gold medal, and suddenly skiing seemed pretty sick again.

Moseley went on to win a silver medal in Big Air at the 1999 Winter X Games, and the Slopestyle title at the 2000 U.S. Open. He returned to the Olympics in 2002, but placed fourth. He no longer competes, but remains an action-sports celebrity.

NATHAN BILOW

FAST FACT
A "yard sale" is a bad wipeout that leaves a skier's gear scattered all over the slope.

97I The first series of professional freestyle skiing events is organized.

1992 Freestyle joins the Olympics. Donna Weinbrecht of the U.S. wins the first gold medal in women's Moguls.

CARL YARBROUGH

Donna Weinbrecht

2002 Jonny Moseley pulls the first off-axis trick in the Winter Games: the dinner roll. Fans love it.

2006 Han Xiaopeng of China wins the men's Aerials event at the Winter Olympics. It is China's first Olympic gold medal on snow.

<GREATEST MOMENT>
FIRST OLYMPIC MOGULS

The first freestyle skiing event to become part of the Winter Olympics was Moguls at the 1992 Games in Albertville, France. Freestyle had been growing in popularity over the past 25 years, especially in the United States. Now it was finally ready for the big time. U.S. skier Donna Weinbrecht cruised down the bumpy run to win the first Olympic gold medal in women's Moguls. Weinbrecht turned out to be the only U.S. skier to win gold at the 1992 Winter Olympics. Her win showed that although the U.S. may have had some catching up to do in Alpine and Nordic events, it would be a leader in freestyle competition.

CARL YARBROUGH

<UP-AND-COMER>
KYE PETERSEN

A regular at Whistler Blackcomb Ski Resort, in British Columbia, Canada, Kye Petersen is an all-around talent. He can jib in the terrain park as well as many of the top pros, and his backcountry skills are awesome for his age — only 16. He's small, just a shade over 5 feet and 100 pounds, but big things are expected from him. Four-time X Games gold medalist Tanner Hall has called Petersen the "future of skiing, for sure." Kye is the son of late freeskiing legend Trevor Petersen. The elder Petersen died in an avalanche while ski-ing the backcountry in the French Alps in 1996. Kye has the bloodlines and the backcountry lines to fulfill Hall's prediction someday soon.

ALEX O'BRIEN

FAST FACT
The texture of freshly groomed snow is called "corduroy" because the long thin lines along the slope resemble the clothing fabric.

SWITCH 720 RODEO TAIL GRAB

TANNER HALL

Jib skiing, where athletes huck tricks on rails, ledges, trees, small jumps — just about anything — is still new. Skiers have been doing it for fewer than 10 years. Still, in that time, one rider has become a legend: Tanner Hall. One of Hall's earlier mind-blowing moves was a switch 720 rodeo tail grab, which he pulled flawlessly to win the 2000 U.S. Freeskiing Open Big Air competition. The trick required Hall to take off from a jump backward and spin two full times with a somersault while grabbing the rear part of his skis, before landing backward again. The trick helped boost Hall's reputation as the man to beat in freeskiing, a position he still commands today.

TOP 10 ATHLETES

1 TANNER HALL, born October 26, 1983, in Kalispell, Montana. A dominant freeskier who rules the park, pipe, and back-country, Hall is an icon to wannabes worldwide. He has won seven Winter X Games medals, including four gold medals. In 2003, he won the World Superpipe Championship and the U.S. Open Slopestyle and Winter X Games Slopestyle events.

Tanner Hall

2 SIMON DUMONT, born July 9, 1986, in Bethel, Maine. A hard-charging high-flier, Dumont always goes big. Sometimes he lands in first place, and sometimes he lands in the hospital. That's what happened when he broke his pelvis and ruptured his spleen after shooting nearly 200 feet off a jump in March 2005. A month before that, he won his second-straight gold medal in Superpipe at the Winter X Games.

3 C.R. JOHNSON, born August 10, 1983, in Truckee, California. An all-around talent, Johnson has built his reputation on big tricks and standout performances in freeskiing films. He was the first to huck a bio 1260 (3 1/2 rotations with a grab) in a contest, and has won two Winter X Games medals. Since December 2005, Johnson has been recovering from serious injuries suffered when young ripper Kye Petersen collided with him during a film shoot.

Grete Eliassen

FLIP McCIRRICK/SHAZAMM/ESPN IMAGES

4 JON OLSSON, born August 17, 1982, in Mora, Sweden. Olsson can ski any terrain with style and skill. He won the Scandinavian Big Mountain Championships in 2004. He has won more Winter X Games medals than any other skier (eight), including a medal in Slopestyle and Superpipe every year since 2002.

5 GRETE ELIASSEN, born September 19, 1986, in Highland Hills, Minnesota. A former ski racer, Eliassen sucessfully made the switch to freeskiing. In 2005 and 2006, she was first in Slopestyle at the U.S. Open and won the gold medal in Superpipe at the Winter X Games both years.

6 SARAH BURKE, born September 3, 1982, in Midland, Ontario, Canada. Burke gets a lot of attention in magazines for her looks, but she has serious game in halfpipe. She won silver medals in the event at the 2005 and 2006 Winter X Games and the 2005 Winter Gravity Games.

7 CHARLES GAGNIER, born July 19, 1985, in Victoriaville, Quebec, Canada. A rail ruler, Gagnier blew up in 2005: He won Slopestyle events at the X Games and U.S. Open, and placed third at the Winter Gravity Games.

8 PEP FUJAS, born November 22, 1982, in Medford, Oregon. A major innovator, Fujas pioneered landing switch stance in powder. He's also a master jibber on rails and ledges. He won silver in Slopestyle at the 2003 Winter X Games, and has earned major props for his stunts in ski films.

9 PETER OLENICK, born February 29, 1984, in Aspen, Colorado. At 6' 1", Olenick towers over his rivals in the park, on the pipe, and on the slopestyle course. He won the Rail Jam at the 2003 U.S. Open. Now a master jibber, he qualified as a little-known freeskier for the Winter X Games in 2004 and won silver in Slopestyle and bronze in Superpipe.

10 SHANE McCONKEY, born December 30, 1969, in Vancouver, British Columbia, Canada. McConkey is the most hard-core freeskier ever. He made his reputation in films with insane rides down steep, powdery terrain. McConkey won the 2000 Winter Gravity Games Big Mountain event, and won silver in Skiercross at the 1999 Winter X Games. In 2003, he pioneered ski BASE jumping, where he rides off cliffs and parachutes to the snow below.

Peter Olenick

WINTER X GAMES RESULTS

MEN

YEAR	EVENT	GOLD	SILVER	BRONZE
2006	Skier X	Lars Lewen, Sweden	Reggie Crist, U.S.	Chris Del Bosco, U.S.
2005	Skier X	Reggie Crist, U.S.	Zach Crist, U.S.	Enak Gavaggio, France
2004	Skier X	Casey Puckett, U.S.	Lars Lewen, Sweden	Reggie Crist, U.S.
2003	Skier X	Lars Lewen, Sweden	Reggie Crist, U.S.	Enak Gavaggio, France
2002	Skier X	Reggie Crist, U.S.	Peter Lind, Sweden	Enak Gavaggio, France
2005	Slopestyle	Charles Gagnier, Canada	Tanner Hall, U.S.	Jon Olsson, Sweden
2004	Slopestyle	Tanner Hall, U.S.	Peter Olenick, U.S.	Jon Olsson, Sweden
2003	Slopestyle	Tanner Hall, U.S.	Pep Fujas, U.S.	Jon Olsson, Sweden
2002	Slopestyle	Tanner Hall, U.S.	C.R. Johnson, U.S.	Jon Olsson, Sweden
2006	Superpipe	Tanner Hall, U.S.	Laurent Favre, France	Simon Dumont, U.S.
2005	Superpipe	Simon Dumont, U.S.	Tanner Hall, U.S.	Jon Olsson, Sweden
2004	Superpipe	Simon Dumont, U.S.	Jon Olsson, Sweden	Peter Olenick, U.S.
2003	Superpipe	Candide Thovex, France	Tanner Hall, U.S.	Jon Olsson, Sweden
2002	Superpipe	Jon Olsson, Sweden	Philippe Larose, Canada	Philippe Poirier, Canada
2006	Best Trick	TJ Schiller, Canada	Charles Gagnier, Canada	Andreas Hatveit, Norway

WOMEN

YEAR	EVENT	GOLD	SILVER	BRONZE
2006	Skier X	Karin Huttary, Austria	Gro Kvinlog, Norway	Ophelie David, France
2005	Skier X	Sanna Tidstrand, Sweden	Karin Huttary, Austria	Magdalena Jonsson, Sweden
2004	Skier X	Karin Huttary, Austria	Aleisha Cline, Canada	Sanna Tidstrand, Sweden
2003	Skier X	Aleisha Cline, Canada	Karin Huttary, Austria	C. Hagen Larsen, Norway
2002	Skier X	Aleisha Cline, Canada	Magdalena Jonsson, Sweden	P. Sherman-Kauf, U.S.
2006	Superpipe	Grete Eliassen, Norway	Sarah Burke, Canada	Marie Martinod-Routin, France
2005	Superpipe	Grete Eliassen, Norway	Sarah Burke, Canada	Kristi Leskinen, U.S.

U.S. FREESKIING OPEN RESULTS

MEN

YEAR	EVENT	GOLD	SILVER	BRONZE
2006	Slopestyle	Corey Vanular, Canada	Sammy Carlson, U.S.	Jon Olsson, Sweden
2005	Slopestyle	Charles Gagnier, Cananda	Tanner Hall, U.S.	Jon Olsson, Sweden
2004	Slopestyle	TJ Schiller, Canada	Henrik Windstedt, Sweden	Tanner Rainville, U.S.
2003	Slopestyle	Tanner Hall, U.S.	Jon Olsson, Sweden	Nick Mercon, U.S.
2002	Slopestyle	Tanner Hall, U.S.	Jon Olsson, Sweden	C.R. Johnson, U.S.
2006	Superpipe	Tanner Hall, U.S.	Loic Collomb-Patton, France	Corey Vanular, Canada
2005	Superpipe	Tanner Hall, U.S.	Sean Field, U.S.	Corey Vanular, Canada
2004	Superpipe	David Crichton, Canada	Tanner Hall, U.S.	Simon Dumont, U.S.
2003	Superpipe	Jon Reedy, U.S.	Greg Tuffelmire, U.S.	Boyd Easley, U.S.
2002	Superpipe	Jon Olsson, Sweden	Candide Thovex, France	David Crighton, Canada
2006	Big Air	TJ Schiller, Canada	Charles Gagnier, Canada	Andreas Haveit, Finland
2005	Big Air	TJ Schiller, Canada	Derek Spong, U.S.	Laurent Favre, France
2004	Big Air	Mickael Deschenaux, Switzerland	TJ Schiller, Canada	Jon Olsson, Sweden
2003	Big Air	Mickael Deschenaux, Switzerland	Tanner Hall, U.S.	Simon Dumont, U.S.
2002	Big Air	C.R. Johnson, U.S.	Tanner Hall, U.S.	David Crighton, Canada
2005	Crossmax	Lars Lewen, Sweden	Enak Gavaggio, France	Tyler Shepherd, U.S.
2004	Skiercross	Tobias Hellman, Sweden	Lars Lewen, Sweden	Reggie Crist, U.S.
2003	Skiercross	Lars Lewen, Sweden	Enak Gavaggio, France	Reggie Crist, U.S.
2002	Skiercross	Reggie Crist, U.S.	Eric Archer, U.S.	Chris Del Bosco, U.S.

WOMEN

YEAR	EVENT	GOLD	SILVER	BRONZE
2006	Slopestyle	Grete Eliassen, Norway	Sarah Burke, Canada	Michelle Parker, U.S.
2005	Slopestyle	Grete Eliassen, Norway	Sarah Burke, Canada	Ashley Battersby, U.S.
2004	Slopestyle	Grete Eliassen, Norway	Virginie Faivre, Switzerland	Ali Van Dorn, U.S.
2003	Slopestyle	Sarah Burke, Canada	Kristi Leskinen, U.S.	Jess Cumming, U.S.
2002	Slopestyle	Sarah Burke, Canada	Jamie Meyers, U.S.	Kristi Leskinen, U.S.

U.S. FREESKIING OPEN RESULTS (CONT.)

YEAR	EVENT	GOLD	SILVER	BRONZE
2006	Superpipe	Sarah Burke, Canada	Jen Hudak, U.S.	Jess Cumming, U.S.
2005	Superpipe	Sarah Burke, Canada	Kristi Leskinen, U.S.	Jen Hudak, U.S.
2004	Superpipe	Marie Martinod-Routin, France	Jamie Sundberg, U.S.	Jen Hudak, U.S.
2003	Superpipe	Marie Martinod-Routin, France	Sarah Burke, Canada	Kim Stacey, U.S.
2002	Superpipe	Jamie Sundberg, U.S.	Kristi Leskinen, U.S.	Sarah Burke, Canada
2005	Crossmax	Ashleigh McIvor, Canada	Anik Demers, Canada	Brett Buckles, U.S.
2004	Skiercross	Aleisha Cline, Canada	Karin Huttary, Austria	Anik Demers, Canada
2003	Skiercross	Karin Huttary, Austria	Ashleigh McIvor, Canada	C. Hagen Larsen, Norway
2002	Skiercross	Katie Shackelford, U.S.	Magdalena Jonsson, Sweden	C. Hagen Larsen, Norway

WINTER GRAVITY GAMES RESULTS

MEN

YEAR	EVENT	GOLD	SILVER	BRONZE
2006	Not held due to Olympic Games			
2005	Skiercross	Casey Puckett, U.S.	Zach Crist, U.S.	Jakub Fiala, U.S.
2005	Superpipe	Corey Vanular, Canada	Andy Woods, U.S.	Simon Dumont, U.S.
2005	Slopestyle	TJ Schiller, Canada	Simon Dumont, U.S.	Charles Gagnier, Canada
2005	Rail Jam	Tim Russell, U.S.	Not awarded	Not awarded

WOMEN

YEAR	EVENT	GOLD	SILVER	BRONZE
2006	Not held due to Olympic Games			
2005	Skiercross	Brett Buckles, U.S.	Valentine Scuotto, France	S.M. Boucher, Canada
2005	Superpipe	Kristi Leskinen, U.S.	Sarah Burke, Canada	Grete Eliassen, Norway
2005	Rail Jam	Grete Eliassen, Norway	Not awarded	Not awarded

WINTER OLYMPICS RESULTS

MEN

YEAR	EVENT	GOLD	SILVER	BRONZE
2006	Moguls	Dale Begg-Smith, Australia	Mikko Ronkainen, Finland	Toby Dawson, U.S.
2002	Moguls	Janne Lahtela, Finland	Travis Mayer, U.S.	Richard Gay, France
1998	Moguls	Jonny Moseley, U.S.	Janne Lahtela, Finland	Sami Mustonen, Finland
1994	Moguls	Jean-Luc Brassard, Canada	Sergei Shupletsov, Russia	Edgar Grospiron, France
1992	Moguls	Edgar Grospiron, France	Olivier Allamand, France	Nelson Carmichael, U.S.
2006	Aerials	Xiaopeng Han, China	Dmitry Dashchinsky, Belarus	Vladimir Lebedev, Russia
2002	Aerials	Alex Valenta, Czech Republic	Joe Pack, U.S.	Alexei Grichin, Belarus
1998	Aerials	Eric Bergoust, U.S.	Sébastien Foucras, France	Dmitri Dashchinsky, Belarus
1994	Aerials	Andreas Schonbachler, Switz.	Philippe Laroche, Canada	Lloyd Langlois, Canada

WOMEN

YEAR	EVENT	GOLD	SILVER	BRONZE
2006	Moguls	Jennifer Heil, Canada	Kari Traa, Norway	Sandra Laoura, France
2002	Moguls	Kari Traa, Norway	Shannon Bahrke, U.S.	Tae Satoya, Japan
1998	Moguls	Tae Satoya, Japan	Tatjana Mittermayer, Germany	Kari Traa, Norway
1994	Moguls	Stine Lise Hattestad, Norway	Elizabeth McIntyre, U.S.	Yelizaveta Kozhevnikova, Russia
1992	Moguls	Donna Weinbrecht, U.S.	Yelizaveta Kozhevnikova, Russia	Stine Lise Hattestad, Norway
2006	Aerials	Evelyne Leu, Switzerland	Nina Li, China	Alisa Camplin, Australia
2002	Aerials	Alisa Camplin, Australia	Veronica Brenner, Canada	Deidra Dionne, Canada
1998	Aerials	Nikki Stone, U.S.	Xu Nannan, China	Colette Brand, Switzerland
1994	Aerials	Lina Cheryazova, Uzbekistan	Marie Lindgren, Sweden	Hilde Synnove Lid, Norway

TOP 10 PLACES TO RIDE

1 **PARK CITY, UTAH.** The home of the 2002 Winter Olympics, Park City Mountain Resort has one of the finest terrain parks around: King's Crown Superpark. Eagle Superpipe, at 22 feet tall, is one of the biggest in the world. Add the Wasatch Mountains backcountry, and you have the reasons why Tanner Hall calls Park City his home base.

2 **LAKE TAHOE.** This area boasts a dozen resorts, in two states — Nevada and California — including Squaw Valley, Sierra-at-Tahoe, Heavenly, and Northstar-at-Tahoe. They offer a variety of terrain for all skill levels. Squaw Valley's moguls and backcountry runs served as a training ground for a young Jonny Moseley.

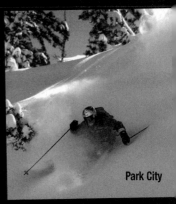

Park City

3 **JACKSON HOLE, WYOMING.** Jackson Hole is one of the toughest resorts to ski in the United States. It has acres of advanced terrain, plus a 4,100-foot vertical drop — one of the largest in North America. Extreme skiers come from around the world to test themselves on the naturally challenging terrain, with its cliffs, bumps, chutes, and deep powder. If you aren't ready for the top of the mountain, stick with the superpipe and terrain park.

4 **ASPEN, COLORADO.** Everything about Aspen is extreme, including the skiing. The world-famous town in the Rocky Mountains offers four resorts: Buttermilk, with a massive superpipe and park, has hosted the Winter X Games for the past five years; Aspen Mountain has good intermediate-to-advanced terrain; Aspen Highlands has a little bit of everything, including super-steep powder runs near the summit; and Snowmass is bigger than the other three combined and has the longest vertical drop (4,400 feet) in the U.S.

Whistler Blackcomb

COURTESY OF WHISTLERBLACKCOMB.COM

5 **WHISTLER BLACKCOMB, BRITISH COLUMBIA, CANADA.** This gigantic resort will host the ski events during the 2010 Winter Olympics in Vancouver. Together, Whistler and Blackcomb mountains have 8,000 acres of terrain, and the longest season in North America. With multiple parks and three pipes, Whistler Blackcomb has something for every level, plus insane backcountry with powder bowls and year-round rides on Palmer Glacier.

Mammoth Mountain

6 MAMMOTH MOUNTAIN, CALIFORNIA. Mammoth is huge, receiving heavy snowfall that lasts into summertime. Its world-famous pipe and parks highlight a wide variety of all-around terrain. Its location — only a few hours from San Diego and Los Angeles — means sometimes the crowds are mammoth, too.

7 MT. BACHELOR, BEND, OREGON. Located on an old volcano, Mt. Bachelor blows away other resorts with its lack of crowds and sunny springtime weather. You can ski all sides of the cone-shaped mountain and explore big backcountry terrain, or stick to the parks (hips, rails, bars, and a fun box) and superpipes.

8 CHAMONIX, FRANCE. The French Alps is the worldwide home of extreme skiing. Chamonix offers steep, gnarly runs, the longest of which is 9,000 feet. Many areas are for experts only. Those who travel off-mountain risk serious consequences: There is the danger of being caught in an avalanche or falling off a cliff.

9 VAL D'ISERE AND TIGNES, FRANCE. The mountains of the French Alps are so large, they stretch between towns, and so do the ski resorts. Val d'Isere and Tignes are connected, resulting in miles of skiable terrain down a 5,000-foot drop. French racing legend Jean-Claude Killy learned to ski on these slopes and helped lure the Winter Olympics here in 1992.

10 STRATTON MOUNTAIN, VERMONT. One of the best halfpipes in North America — which hosts the annual U.S. Open Snowboarding Championships — plus five parks make Stratton a playground for freeskiing nuts. The wide, gentle slopes offer a good place to learn or just cruise.

CHAPTER 6

SNOWBOARDING

Snowboarders were not allowed on the
mountains in the sport's early days. Today,
boarders outnumber skiers on the slopes.

Shaun White has
won eight Winter
X Games medals.

JEFF CURTES

N o one knows for sure when the first snowboard was built. But one of the first successful "snowboards" was created on Christmas Day in 1965, in a garage in Muskegon, Michigan.

An engineer named Sherman Poppen had watched his daughter Wendy try to stand on her sled while riding down a hill. Inspired, he screwed two skis together and created the "Snurfer." Poppen's wife came up with the name by combining the words *surfer* and *snow*.

Snurfers were made of plastic and had a rope attached to the front for riders to hang on to. Thousands of them were sold during the next 10 years all over the country.

The Snurfer inspired the modern snowboard. Many of the inventors who would go on to create the first snowboards in the mid-1970's rode Snurfers as kids. These pioneers would produce equipment with a major design change: bindings to strap the feet to the board.

The Rise of Burton

Surfer Dimitrije Milovich was one of those pioneers. In 1970, he began creating snowboards shaped like surfboards, but with metal edges similar to those found on skis. The next year, Milovich received a patent for his design, which he called the Winterstick. By 1975, he began manufacturing the Winterstick in Utah.

Jake Burton Carpenter grew up on Long Island, outside New York City, riding Snurfers during the winter. In 1977, after graduating from New York University, he moved to Vermont and pursued his dream of creating a new sport — snowboarding. With the $120,000 that he had inherited from his grandmother, Carpenter began making his boards out of wood. He loaded them into his station wagon and drove to local ski shops to sell them. Often he performed demonstrations, showing how the boards should be ridden. This was the beginning of Burton Snowboards, which is now the world's largest snowboard maker.

Meanwhile in California, a pro skateboarder named

Janna Meyen has won four straight Winter X Games Slopestyle gold medals.

SCOTTSERFAS.COM

Tom Sims teamed with surfer Bob Webber, who had been experimenting with what he called "skiboard" designs. Together, they created the Sims Skiboard, with a plastic molded bottom and a skateboard deck mounted on top. With several manufacturers working across the country, snowboarding began to increase in popularity.

Early Contests

In 1979, Snurfers were still more popular than snowboards. At an annual Snurfer contest in Muskegon, Michigan, Carpenter showed up with his boards and tried to enter. Many Snurfer contestants complained about his unusual equipment. Carpenter was allowed to compete, but in a special "open" class. As the only entrant, he won first place.

The first small snowboard contest was held in

Ross Powers is a two-time U.S. Open Halfpipe champion.

Leadville, Colorado, in April 1981. The following year, professional Snurfer Paul Graves organized the first major contest, the National Snowsurfing Championships in Woodstock, Vermont. The event featured slalom and downhill competition between snowboarders and Snurfers from all over the country. *Sports Illustrated* and *Good Morning America* covered the event.

East Versus West

In 1983, Carpenter organized the National Snowboarding Championships in Snow Valley, Vermont. The event would eventually become the U.S. Open Snowboarding Championships, the sport's longest-running contest. That same year, Sims founded the World Snowboarding Championships in Lake Tahoe, California. Two distinct snowboard scenes were developing, one in the Lake Tahoe area of California and Nevada, and the other in Vermont. Together, they would help the sport grow nationwide.

A major design innovation also appeared in 1983: the highback binding. This came up behind the rider's boot and offered more support. It allowed shredders to carve better on hard-packed snow. Up to this point, few ski resorts permitted snowboarding on their slopes. But in 1984, Stratton Mountain in Vermont opened its slopes to shredders for the first time. Out west, Donner Ski Ranch in California allowed boarding on a limited basis.

Going Mainstream

In 1985, several things helped snowboarding shift from a fringe activity to the mainstream. The first snowboarding magazine, *Absolutely Radical*, was published. Also, metal edges were introduced on the Burton Performer and Sims 1500 FE models, allowing for more controlled turning. Sims also unveiled the first pro model for Terry Kidwell, a freestyle rider from Lake Tahoe who was among the first boarders to pull aerials. Finally, Sims performed as a stunt double for Roger Moore in the movie *A View to a Kill*, which featured James Bond escaping from bad-guy skiers on a

FAST FACT

At the 2001 Arctic Challenge, Heikki Sorsa of Finland set the world record for highest air with a 28-foot blast above a quarterpipe.

snowboard. It was clear that snowboarding was no fad.

Snowboarding was now entering its modern age. In 1987, the snowboarding company Barfoot created the first twin tip symmetrical (or balanced) freestyle board design. Halfpipe ramps, which were first ridden in the Lake Tahoe area and debuted in competition at the 1983 World Snowboarding Championships, were becoming a fixture at most contests.

The Sport's New Stars

The sport's first freestyle stars were emerging from the West Coast. The two biggest were Shaun Palmer, a brash kid from San Diego, California, and Craig Kelly, a Mt. Baker, Washington, native. Kelly would soon set the early standard for shredding style. He won the Slalom event for the first time at the U.S. Open in 1987. The Halfpipe event debuted the following year, and he placed third. In 1989, Kelly won the first of back-to-back Halfpipe titles.

The next star of the growing freestyle movement was Terje Haakonsen from Norway. He was a naturally gifted rider who raised snowboarding standards with his soaring, stylish aerials. Haakonsen routinely blasted 10 feet above the lip of the halfpipe when his peers managed only half that distance. He won the U.S. Open Halfpipe title three times from 1992 to 1995 and finished second in 1997 and 1998.

Olympic Exposure

Meanwhile, the governing body for competitive and Olympic skiing, the Fédération Internationale de Ski (FIS), officially recognized snowboarding in 1993. That paved the way for the sport's inclusion in the 1998 Winter Olympics in Nagano, Japan. The Winter X Games, which included snowboarding, debuted in 1997 at Snow Summit in Big Bear Lake, California. Suddenly, snowboarding was becoming a more commercial sport.

Some riders weren't sure they liked that. Several boarders, including Haakonsen, were unhappy about the FIS taking control of snowboarding. He would later boycott the Olympics in protest.

Growing Fast

Still, the exposure of these events gave snowboarding a huge boost. At the 1998 Winter Olympics, boarders competed in Halfpipe and Giant Slalom. After the Games, people rushed out to try snowboarding. It

soon became the fastest-growing sport in the United States.

The level of tricks continued to grow, too. A "jib" movement emerged, in which boarders took to the streets, sliding on handrails like street skaters. Pros such as JP Walker and Jeremy Jones showcased this type of riding in snowboarding magazines.

Danny Kass is known for his technical skills in the pipe.

TOM ZIKAS

A New Crew

Women's snowboarding also took off. There had always been a noticeable difference between the skill levels of men's and women's riders. But a younger, aggressive generation of riders rose up to close the gap. Tara Dakides blazed a trail in Big Air and Slopestyle. In the pipe, Kelly Clark flew high and spun flawless 540s. They were joined by Gretchen Bleiler, Hannah Teter, Elena Hight, and Torah Bright. These women are so talented that they wouldn't look out of place competing against the men.

Millions of viewers watched the Halfpipe event at the 2002 Winter Olympics, fueling the American public's obsession with the sport. It helped that Americans won all three medals in the men's Halfpipe and the gold in women's Halfpipe. Since then, the sport has continued to surge, and now — with seven million participants — it has surpassed skiing's popularity in the United States.

Today, snowboarders are welcome at nearly every resort, and many cater to boarders with halfpipes and terrain parks. Lately, however, there is a movement growing toward developing all-mountain skills. Many top pros are exploring backcountry terrain where no ski lifts go. Travis Rice and Jeremy Jones are two pros who are pushing the level of this type of riding. But instead of having to hike up the mountains as the early riders did 25 years ago, these stars reach the top by helicopter.

<UP-AND-COMER>
HANNAH TETER

Hannah Teter hails from Belmont, Vermont, and is the younger sister of pro boarders Abe and Elijah Teter. She rose up through the junior levels of the U.S. Open, finishing second in the Halfpipe at the Girl's Junior Jam in 2001. The next year, she moved up to the pro ranks and placed second in women's Slopestyle at the U.S. Open.

Teter has an aggressive style in the pipe and soars nearly as high as the men. She has pushed the progression of women's riding. In 2003, Teter added the 900 to her bag of tricks and finished third in Halfpipe and Slopestyle at the Winter X Games and the U.S. Open. She won the Superpipe at the Winter X Games in 2004. She went even bigger at the 2006 Winter Olympics, winning the gold medal in Halfpipe at age 18.

DEAN BLOTTO

TIME LINE

1965 Sherman Poppen invents the Snurfer by bolting two skis together side by side.

1970 Surfer Dimitrije Milovich develops a snowboard with metal edges.

1975 Dimitrije Milovich begins manufacturing his "Wintersticks" in Utah. His early designs are based on surfboards.

NECESSARY OBJECTS

- **SNOWBOARD:** Boards are made of fiberglass with a wood core. The top sheet usually has a graphic printed on it. Snowboards have metal edges, which allow them to carve, or turn. There are two main types of boards: freeride and freestyle. Freeriding boards are the more popular and versatile. They can be used on most mountain terrain, including parks and halfpipes. Freeride boards have a directional design, which means that the tail is narrower, shorter, and flatter than the tip. These boards are designed to be ridden forward, but can also be ridden switch stance. Freestyle boards are used to perform tricks in halfpipes and parks. They are shorter, lighter, and have more flexibility than freeride boards. However, they are slower and do not turn as well. Freestyle boards are symmetrical, meaning the tip and tail are the same size and shape. This permits both regular and switch-stance riding.

  Boards come in a variety of sizes, depending on a rider's height, weight, and foot size. They range from 90 centimeters (about 3 feet) in length for a kid's freestyle model to 170 centimeters (5 ½ feet) for a men's freeride board. Talk to an expert at a snowboard shop before you buy one.

- **BINDINGS:** Bindings strap your feet to the board. There are two main types. The most popular type is strap-in bindings, which are worn with a soft, comfortable boot. The boot steps into the binding and is strapped down tight. Most freestyle and freeride boarders use these bindings because they provide more control and comfort. Step-in bindings are the most convenient. The rider, wearing soft or hard boots, simply steps down onto the binding, which then clicks into place. The drawbacks to these bindings are a loss of control and their tendency to come undone, especially during freestyle sessions.

- **HELMET:** Helmets are always a good idea, but are especially necessary for freestyle riders in parks and pipes. Trying tricks without protecting your head is not smart. Make sure helmets are CEN-rated (Comité Européen de Normalisation) for safety and proper fit. Most helmets now come with a removable, washable liner and earflaps to keep you warm as well as safe.

- **BOOTS:** A good pair of boots will keep your feet warm and comfortable. Snowboard boots have an outer shell with laces — and sometimes straps — and an interior liner that laces up to keep feet toasty and dry. Most soft boots can be used for strap-in bindings, but only certain types of step-in boots work with step-in bindings. Boots are big and clunky and usually run a size bigger than your shoe size. Make sure they fit right.

1977 Jake Burton Carpenter moves to Vermont and begins making prototypes for what become Burton snowboards.

Jake Burton Carpenter

NANCIE BATTAGLIA

1979 At the annual Snurfer contest in Muskegon, Michigan, Jake Burton Carpenter introduces his handmade snowboard equipment. He is the only competitor without a Snurfer, so he competes in an "open" division. Carpenter wins because he is the sole contestant.

1981 The first modern snowboard contest is held in Leadville, Colorado.

<GREATEST MOMENT>
SNOWBOARDING AT THE 1998 WINTER OLYMPICS

Snowboarding began to surge in popularity in the mid-1980's. But skiing still ruled the slopes, and many resorts refused to allow snowboarders on their mountains. Nevertheless, boarding continued to grow. By the early 1990's, most resorts opened their runs to snowboarders, forcing skiers to share the snow. The biggest boost to snowboarding occurred when two of the sport's disciplines (Halfpipe and Giant Slalom) made their debut at the 1998 Winter Olympics in Nagano, Japan. Gian Simmen of Switzerland and Nicola

Thost of Germany won the men's and women's Halfpipe. Ross Rebagliati of Canada and Karine Ruby of France won the men's and women's Giant Slalom. It was the first glimpse of snowboarding for many viewers. As a result, many people rushed to try this daring sport. Four years later, by the time of the 2002 Winter Olympics, snowboarding was the fastest-growing sport in the United States. Today, more people in the U.S. snowboard than ski, according to the National Sporting Goods Association.

NATHAN BILOW/ALLSPORT

FAST FACT

Snowboarders (and surfers and skateboarders) who stand with their left foot forward on the board ride "regular foot." A rider is "goofy foot" if he or she stands with the right foot forward.

TIME LINE

1982 Pro Snurfer Paul Graves organizes the National Snowsurfing Championships in Woodstock, Vermont. The event features snowboarders and Snurfers competing together in Slalom and Downhill.

1983 Jake Burton Carpenter organizes the National Snowboarding Championships in Snow Valley, Vermont. Tom Sims holds the World Snowboarding Championships in Lake Tahoe, California.

Mt. Baker
GWYN HOWAT

1985 Mt. Baker, Washington, holds the first Mt. Baker Legendary Banked Slalom a race that awards rolls of Duct Tape to the winners.

GROUNDBREAKING TRICK
WOMEN MASTER THE 900

A major breakthrough in women's halfpipe riding occurred in January 2003. Three women "dialed 9" in competition at a Grand Prix event in Breckenridge, Colorado. Hannah Teter, Elena Hight, and Lindsey Jacobellis all busted a 900 (2½-rotation) spin, marking the first time the move had ever been done by a woman in competition. The 900 was already an established trick in men's riding. When the women nailed it, the trick upped the respect for the women and closed the gender gap. Teter's 900 was the tightest, and she won the event that day. Hight seemed to have the spin to go for another half-rotation. And Jacobellis threw her 900 while she was 10 feet in the air. With so many women now throwing the 900 with style, it won't be long before the 1080 (three full rotations) is unveiled.

1986 Stratton Mountain in Vermont becomes the first resort to offer snowboard instruction.

1987 Snowboard manufacturer Barfoot debuts the first twin tip freestyle model with an identical nose and tail, the first European World Championships are held, and *Transworld Snowboarding* publishes its first issue.

Transworld Snowboarding

GUY MOTIL

1988 The United States Amateur Snowboarding Association (USASA) is founded with a $500 donation from *Transworld Snowboarding*. It is the sport's first sanctioning body for amateur events.

THE BASIC TRICKS

METHOD AIR▶

This is a tweaked-out backside air. The rider's front hand grabs the board's heel edge. With the rider's knees bent, the board is pulled up behind the rider, so that the body becomes parallel to the ground.

FRONTSIDE (INDY) AIR▲

An air where the rider's rear hand grabs the frontside edge of the board between the bindings. Regular-foot riders use the right hand; goofy-foot riders use the left.

RAILSLIDE/ BOARDSLIDE▶

The rider turns 90 degrees to slide the rails (edges) of the board on any surface, such as a fallen tree, a picnic table, handrails, or the lip of a halfpipe.

TIME LINE

Welcome, boarder

1989 Many of the biggest ski resorts around the nation finally welcome snowboarders onto their slopes.

1990 Breckenridge Ski Corporation announces plans for the Snowboarding Hall of Fame to house the sport's historic artifacts. Vail Ski Resort creates the first "snowboard park."

1993 The Fédération Internationale de Ski (FIS), skiing's international and Olympi organizing body, votes to recognize snowboarding

INNOVATOR

TERJE HAAKONSEN

Growing up in the far northern Scandinavian country of Norway, Terje Haakonsen was accustomed to being on top of the world. That's exactly where he found himself shortly after arriving on the pro snowboard scene in the early 1990's.

Haakonsen was known for his huge, soaring airs, which he performed flawlessly. In 1992, at age 18, he took over the halfpipe discipline. Haakonsen won every World Cup event he entered that year — 14 in all — including the U.S. Open. While his fellow competitors were floating 5 feet out of the pipe, he would routinely fly 10 feet high. Haakonsen was U.S. Open champ in 1993 and 1995. But despite his success, he eventually grew disillusioned with competitive snowboarding. Haakonsen famously boycotted the 1998 Winter Olympics because he felt it was a big commercial event with too many rules. By then he rode only in select events, including the Arctic Challenge, which he founded in 1999.

Organized by riders, the Arctic Challenge is held in Norway and attracts the world's best snowboarders — by invitation only. The Challenge features a quarterpipe competition that hurls riders to insane heights.

Haakonsen is more than a high flier, however; he rules on the ground, too. In 2004, he won the Mt. Baker Legendary Banked Slalom title, demonstrating his versatility. It was the sixth time he had won the event.

Today, the name *Terje* commands instant respect among snowboarders everywhere. His influence can still be seen at any contest in which riders attempt to go huge.

JANIS PIPARS

1995 Legend Terje Haakonsen of Norway wins his third and final Halfpipe title at the U.S. Open.

1997 The Winter X Games debut at Snow Summit Mountain Resort in Big Bear Lake, California.

The first Winter X Games

LARRY DORTCH /SAN BERNARDINO COUNTY SUN/AP

< L E G E N D >
SHAUN PALMER

The legend of Shaun Palmer is mountain-sized. He is one of the most talented and versatile boarders ever to strap in. Palmer began riding during the early 1980's near his home in South Lake Tahoe, California. Before snowboarding was allowed at ski resorts, Palmer and friends hiked up the sides of nearby mountains to ride.

As snowboarding began to take off during the mid-1980's, Palmer was ready. In March 1985, at age 16, he won the Junior World Championships in Slalom and Halfpipe. Over the next 15 years, Palmer ruled three disciplines: halfpipe, snowboardcross, and slalom. Meanwhile, his wild hairdos and tattoos helped shape the punk-rock attitude of the sport.

In 1986 and 1987, Palmer won the Mt. Baker Legendary Banked Slalom. In 1989, he won the first of back-to-back world championships in Halfpipe. Palmer's ultracompetitive attitude could not be contained to one sport, however. In 1996, he gave pro mountain biking a try. He won the Slalom and placed second in the Downhill at the world championships that year. For the next three years, Palmer proved he was one of the world's best mountain bikers. With that mission accomplished, he soon switched to motorcycles and raced pro motocross.

Meanwhile, Palmer won gold medals in Snowboardcross at the Winter X Games three years in a row (1997-99). By then, he was winding down his competitive career. He had founded his own company, Palmer Snowboards, in 1995. In 2001, Activision launched the video game series, *Shaun Palmer's Pro Snowboarder*. Now mostly retired from competition, Palmer has left big tracks to fill.

SHAZAMM/ESPN IMAGES

━┥TIME LINE┝━

1998 Snowboarding debuts at the Winter Olympics in Nagano, Japan. Ross Rebagliati of Canada and Karine Ruby of France win gold medals in Giant Slalom. Gian Simmen of Switzerland and Nicola Thost of Germany win gold in Halfpipe.

Ross Rebagliati

ALEXANDER ZEMLIANICHENKO/AP

2002 At the Winter Olympics in Salt Lake City, Utah, Ross Powers and Kelly Clark of the United States win gold in Halfpipe, and Philipp Schoch of Switzerland and Isabelle Blanc of France win gold in Giant Slalom.

<UP-AND-COMER>
LUKE MITRANI

Luke Mitrani grew up in Stratton, Vermont, and began snowboarding at age 6. He started competing at age 9 and won every contest he entered. By age 11, Mitrani became the youngest rider to advance to the quarterfinals in the Halfpipe at the U.S. Open. Pulling huge airs for such a half-pint, he won the Halfpipe in the 2002 Boy's Junior Jam at the U.S. Open. The following year, he became the youngest member of the U.S. National Snowboard Team. Now age 15 and a pro, he's looking to break into the ranks of the top men's halfpipe riders in the world.

DEAN BLOTTO GRAY

FAST FACT

"Jib" boarding is inspired by street skateboarding. Jib riding includes pulling flatland tricks and sliding on rails and tree limbs.

2003 Hannah Teter, Lindsey Jacobellis, and Elena Hight each nail a 900 at a Grand Prix event in Breckenridge, Colorado. It is the first time the move has been done by a woman in competition.

Danny Kass

ALDEN PELLETT/AP

2006 United States snowboarders win three gold medals (by Shaun White, Hanna Teeter, and Seth Wescott) and three silver medals (by Danny Kass, Gretchen Bleiler, and Lindsey Jacobellis) at the Winter Olympics.

TOP 10 ATHLETES

Shaun White

1 SHAUN WHITE, born September 3, 1986, in San Diego, California. White is a pro snowboarder *and* a pro skateboarder. He won a silver medal at the 2005 X Games in skateboard Vert to go with his eight Winter X medals (six of which are gold). White turned pro in snowboarding at age 12. He climbed to the top in slopestyle and superpipe with a trinity of talent: technical tricks, smooth style, and major amplitude. He hit new heights with a gold medal in Halfpipe at the 2006 Winter Olympics.

2 DANNY KASS, born September 21, 1982, in Pompton Plains, New Jersey. Kass has been the man to beat in the pipe since emerging in 2001. That year, he won the Winter X Games, U.S. Open, and every major contest he entered. Kass continues to push the progression of technical tricks in halfpipe. He won the silver medal at the 2002 and 2006 Winter Olympics and a record fourth U.S. Open title in 2005. Kass has shown serious skills in slopestyle, too, winning silver medals at the Winter X Games in 2004 and 2005, and bronze in 2006.

3 ROSS POWERS, born February 10, 1979, in South Londonderry, Vermont. Powers is a high-flying pipe master. He first competed at the U.S. Open as a 9-year-old, and won the event in 1999 and 2003. Powers is the only rider to medal at the first two Olympics in which the sport appeared (bronze in 1998 and gold in 2002).

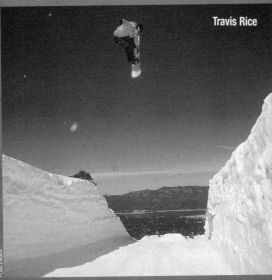

Travis Rice

TOM ZIKAS

4 TRAVIS RICE, born October 9, 1982, in Jackson Hole, Wyoming. Rice is fearless and will try anything. He competes in all disciplines, but is known as a master of slopestyle and backcountry runs. In 2002, Rice won gold in Slopestyle at the Winter Games and placed second in Slopestyle at the U.S. Open. He earned bronze in Slopestyle at the Winter X Games in 2005. His most memorable moves, however, come while launching hundreds of feet through the backcountry in snowboarding videos.

5 KELLY CLARK, born July 26, 1983, in Newport, Rhode Island. Clark exploded out of the halfpipe in 2002. She won the Winter Olympics, Winter X Games, and U.S. Open with huge air, smooth style, and a slew of 540s. Clark is always a threat to win in the pipe. She was a repeat winner at the U.S. Open in 2004, and at the Winter X Games in 2006.

6 GRETCHEN BLEILER, born April 10, 1981, in Toledo, Ohio. Bleiler had a remarkable year in 2005. She won Superpipe at the Winter X Games and Gravity Games, and Halfpipe at the U.S. Open. A fan favorite, Bleiler won a silver medal in Halfpipe at the 2006 Winter Olympics.

Gretchen Bleiler

TOM ZIKAS

7 LINDSEY JACOBELLIS, born August 19, 1985, in Roxbury, Connecticut. Jacobellis is one of the most versatile riders in the world. She is a triple threat in halfpipe, snowboardcross, and slopestyle. In 2005, Jacobellis won the World and U.S. championships, and a third straight Winter X Games gold, all in Snowboardcross. She won silver in that event at the 2006 Winter Olympics.

8 JEREMY JONES, born January 2, 1976, in Salt Lake City, Utah. Jones can rule a park or city streetscape, or wow with gnarly riding in ungroomed powder off the beaten track. Every year, new video footage of him raises the bar for snowboarding. The video *Shakedown* highlights his latest rail assaults.

9 JP WALKER, born October 16, 1976, in Salt Lake City, Utah. Walker rules the rails and practically invented jibbing by riding around Salt Lake City like a street skater on snow. He seldom enters contests, instead beefing up his reputation with heavy moves in videos.

JP Walker

ANDYWRIGHTPHOTO.COM

10 ANTTI AUTTI, born March 15, 1985, in Rovaniemi, Finland. Autti surprised the world's top halfpipe riders in 2005. He won the gold medal in Superpipe at the Winter X Games (the first non-American to win the event) and was second at the U.S. Open. Autti's back-to-back 1080s (three full rotations) in the pipe make him tough to beat. He's versatile, too. In 2005, he placed first in the Straight Air session at the Arctic Challenge and second in Slopestyle at the Winter Gravity Games.

WINTER X GAMES RESULTS

MEN

YEAR	EVENT	GOLD	SILVER	BRONZE
2006	Slopestyle	Shaun White, U.S.	Andreas Wiig, Norway	Danny Kass, U.S.
2005	Slopestyle	Shaun White, U.S.	Danny Kass, U.S.	Travis Rice, U.S.
2004	Slopestyle	Shaun White, U.S.	Danny Kass, U.S.	Andreas Wiig, Norway
2003	Slopestyle	Shaun White, U.S.	Jussi Oksanen, Finland	Jimi Tomer, U.S.
2002	Slopestyle	Travis Rice, U.S.	Shaun White, U.S.	Todd Richards, U.S.
2001	Slopestyle	Kevin Jones, U.S.	Todd Richards, U.S.	Jussi Oksanen, Finland
2000	Slopestyle	Kevin Jones, U.S.	Todd Richards, U.S.	Peter Line, U.S.
1999	Slopestyle	Peter Line, U.S.	Kevin Jones, U.S.	Jimmy Halopoff, U.S.
1998	Slopestyle	Ross Powers, U.S.	Kevin Jones, U.S.	Rob Kingwill, U.S.
1997	Slopestyle	Daniel Franck, Norway	Jimmy Halopoff, U.S.	Bryan Iguchi, U.S.
2006	Snowboarder X	Nate Holland, U.S.	Marco Huser, Switzerland	Jason Hale, U.S.
2005	Snowboarder X	Xavier de le Rue, France	Seth Wescott, U.S.	Marco Huser, Switzerland
2004	Snowboarder X	Ueli Kestenholz, Switzerland	Seth Wescott, U.S.	Xavier de le Rue, France
2003	Snowboarder X	Ueli Kestenholz, Switzerland	Xavier de le Rue, France	Michael Rosengren, U.S.
2002	Snowboarder X	Philippe Conte, Switzerland	Seth Wescott, U.S.	Berti Denervaud, Switzerland
2001	Snowboarder X	Scott Gaffney, Canada	Mark Schulz, U.S.	Seth Wescott, U.S.
2000	Snowboarder X	Drew Neilson, Canada	Scott Gaffney, Canada	Jason Ford, U.S.
1999	Snowboarder X	Shaun Palmer, U.S.	Drew Neilson, Canada	Scott Gaffney, Canada
1998	Snowboarder X	Shaun Palmer, U.S.	Jason Brown, U.S.	Seth Wescott, U.S.
1997	Snowboarder X	Shaun Palmer, U.S.	Berti Denervaud, Switzerland	Mike Basich, U.S.
2006	Superpipe	Shaun White, U.S.	Mason Aguirre, U.S.	Scotty Lago, U.S.
2005	Superpipe	Antti Autti, Finland	Andy Finch, U.S.	Danny Kass, U.S.
2004	Superpipe	Steve Fisher, U.S.	Danny Kass, U.S.	Keir Dillon, U.S.
2003	Superpipe	Shaun White, U.S.	Danny Kass, U.S.	Markku Koski, Finland
2002	Superpipe	J.J. Thomas, U.S.	Shaun White, U.S.	Keir Dillon, U.S.
2001	Superpipe	Danny Kass, U.S.	Tommy Czeschin, U.S.	Ross Powers, U.S.
2000	Superpipe	Todd Richards, U.S.	Ross Powers, U.S.	Tommy Czeschin, U.S.
1999	Halfpipe	Jimi Scott, U.S.	Mike Michalchuk, Canada	Luke Wynen, U.S.
1998	Halfpipe	Ross Powers, U.S.	Guillaume Chastagnol, France	Todd Richards, U.S.
1997	Halfpipe	Todd Richards, U.S.	Daniel Franck, Norway	Fabien Rohrer, Switzerland
2001	Big Air	Jussi Oksanen, Finland	Todd Richards, U.S.	Josh Dirksen, U.S.
2000	Big Air	Peter Line, U.S.	Jason Borgstede, U.S.	Kevin Jones, U.S.
1999	Big Air	Kevin Sansalone, Canada	Peter Line, U.S.	Kevin Jones, U.S.
1998	Big Air	Jason Borgstede, U.S.	Ryan W. Williams, U.S.	Kevin Jones, U.S.
1997	Big Air	Jimmy Halopoff, U.S.	Steve Adkins, U.S.	Bjorn Leines, U.S.

WOMEN

YEAR	EVENT	GOLD	SILVER	BRONZE
2006	Slopestyle	Janna Meyen, U.S.	Hana Beaman, U.S.	Jamie Anderson, U.S.
2005	Slopestyle	Janna Meyen, U.S.	Silvia Mittermueller, Germany	Natasza Zurek, Canada
2004	Slopestyle	Janna Meyen, U.S.	Tara Dakides, U.S.	Jessica Dalpiaz, U.S.
2003	Slopestyle	Janna Meyen, U.S.	Hana Beaman, U.S.	Lindsey Jacobellis, U.S.
2002	Slopestyle	Tara Dakides, U.S.	Janna Meyen, U.S.	Barrett Christy, U.S.
2001	Slopestyle	Jaime MacLeod, U.S.	Shannon Dunn, U.S.	Marni Yamada, U.S.
2000	Slopestyle	Tara Dakides, U.S.	Jaime MacLeod, U.S.	Barrett Christy, U.S.
1999	Slopestyle	Tara Dakides, U.S.	Barrett Christy, U.S.	Jaime MacLeod, U.S.
1998	Slopestyle	Jennie Waara, Sweden	Barrett Christy, U.S.	Aurelie Sayres, U.S.
1997	Slopestyle	Barrett Christy, U.S.	Cara-Beth Burnside, U.S.	Jennie Waara, Sweden
2006	Snowboarder X	Majlle Ricker, Canada	Joanie Anderson, U.S.	Claudia Haeusermann, Switzerland
2005	Snowboarder X	Lindsey Jacobellis, U.S.	Erin Simmons, Canada	Karine Ruby, France
2004	Snowboarder X	Lindsey Jacobellis, U.S.	Karine Ruby, France	Yvonne Mueller, Switzerland
2003	Snowboarder X	Lindsey Jacobellis, U.S.	Tanja Frieden, Switzerland	Yvonne Mueller, Switzerland
2002	Snowboarder X	Ine Poetzl, Austria	Erin Simmons, Canada	Tanja Frieden, Switzerland

WINTER X GAMES RESULTS (CONT.)

WOMEN

YEAR	EVENT	GOLD	SILVER	BRONZE
2001	Snowboarder X	Line Oestvold, Norway	Erin Simmons, Canada	Amy Johnson, U.S.
2000	Snowboarder X	Leslee Olson, U.S.	Carlee Baker, Canada	Line Oestvold, Norway
1999	Snowboarder X	Maelle Ricker, Canada	Leslee Olson, U.S.	Candice Drouin, Canada
1998	Snowboarder X	Tina Dixon, U.S.	Corrie Rudishauser, U.S.	Katrina Warnick, U.S.
1997	Snowboarder X	Jennie Waara, Sweden	Hillary Maybery, U.S.	Aurelie Sayres, U.S.
2006	Superpipe	Kelly Clark, U.S.	Torah Bright, Australia	Soko Yamaoka, Japan
2005	Superpipe	Gretchen Bleiler, U.S.	Doriane Vidal, France	Hannah Teter, U.S.
2004	Superpipe	Hannah Teter, U.S.	Kelly Clark, U.S.	Doriane Vidal, France
2003	Superpipe	Gretchen Bleiler, U.S.	Kelly Clark, U.S.	Hannah Teter, U.S.
2002	Superpipe	Kelly Clark, U.S.	Stine Brun Kjeldaas, Norway	Natasza Zurek, Canada
2001	Superpipe	Shannon Dunn, U.S.	Natasza Zurek, Canada	Fabienne Reuteler, Switzerland
2000	Superpipe	Stine Brun Kjeldaas, Norway	Barrett Christy, U.S.	Natasza Zurek, Canada
1999	Halfpipe	Michelle Taggart, U.S.	Shannon Dunn, U.S.	Cara-Beth Burnside, U.S.
1998	Halfpipe	Cara-Beth Burnside, U.S.	Michelle Taggart, U.S.	Nicola Thost, Germany
1997	Halfpipe	Shannon Dunn, U.S.	Jennie Waara, Sweden	Nicole Angelrath, Switzerland
2001	Big Air	Tara Dakides, U.S.	Barrett Christy, U.S.	Jenna Murano, U.S.
2000	Big Air	Tara Dakides, U.S.	Leah Wagner, Canada	Jessica Dalpiaz, U.S.
1999	Big Air	Barrett Christy, U.S.	Tara Dakides, U.S.	Janet Matthews, Canada
1998	Big Air	Tina Basich, U.S.	Barrett Christy, U.S.	Tara Zwink, U.S.
1997	Big Air	Barrett Christy, U.S.	Tara Zwink, U.S.	Tina Basich, U.S.

X GAMES RESULTS

MEN

YEAR	EVENT	GOLD	SILVER	BRONZE
1999	Big Air	Peter Line, U.S.	Ben Hinkley, U.S.	Chris Engelsman, U.S.
1998	Big Air	Kevin Jones, U.S.	Ben Hinkley, U.S.	Jim Rippey, U.S.
1997	Big Air	Peter Line, U.S.	Kevin Jones, U.S.	Jason Borgstede, U.S.

WOMEN

YEAR	EVENT	GOLD	SILVER	BRONZE
1999	Big Air	Barrett Christy, U.S.	Tina Dixon, U.S.	Janet Matthews, Canada
1998	Big Air	Janet Matthews, Canada	Tina Basich, U.S.	Tina Dixon, U.S.
1997	Big Air	Tina Dixon, U.S.	Hillary Maybery, U.S.	Shelly Ueckert, U.S.

GRAVITY GAMES RESULTS

MEN

YEAR	EVENT	GOLD	SILVER	BRONZE
2006	Not held due to Olympic Games			
2005	Snowboardcross	Xavier de le Rue, France	Jason Smith, U.S.	Mike Rosengren, U.S.
2005	Slopestyle	Chad Otterstrom, U.S.	Antti Autti, Finland	Wyatt Caldwell, U.S.
2005	Superpipe	Crispin Lipscomb, Canada	Danny Davis, U.S.	Risto Mattila, Finland
2005	Rail Jam	Chad Otterstrom, U.S.	Not awarded	Not awarded

WOMEN

YEAR	EVENT	GOLD	SILVER	BRONZE
2006	Not held due to Olympic Games			
2005	Snowboardcross	Leslee Olson, U.S.	Marni Yamada, U.S.	Jordan Karlinski, U.S.
2005	Slopestyle	Janna Meyen, U.S.	Silvia Mittermueller, Germany	Izumi Amaike, Japan
2005	Superpipe	Gretchen Bleiler, U.S.	Hannah Teter, U.S.	Elena Hight, U.S.
2005	Rail Jam	Leanne Pelosi, Canada	Not awarded	Not awarded

U.S. OPEN SNOWBOARDING CHAMPIONSHIPS RESULTS

MEN

YEAR	EVENT	GOLD	SILVER	BRONZE
2006	Halfpipe	Shaun White, U.S.	Danny Davis, U.S.	Mason Aguirre, U.S.
2005	Halfpipe	Danny Kass, U.S.	Steve Fisher, U.S.	Antti Autti, Finland
2004	Halfpipe	Danny Kass, U.S.	Steve Fisher, U.S.	Keir Dillon, U.S.
2003	Halfpipe	Ross Powers, U.S.	Kazuhiro Kokubo, Japan	Daniel Franck, Norway
2002	Halfpipe	Danny Kass, U.S.	Markku Koski, Finland	Keir Dillon, U.S.
2001	Halfpipe	Danny Kass, U.S.	Abe Teter, U.S.	Daniel Franck, Norway
2000	Halfpipe	Guillaume Morisset, Canada	Ross Powers, U.S.	Xavier Hoffman, Germany
1999	Halfpipe	Ross Powers, U.S.	Xavier Hoffman, Germany	Tommy Czeschin, U.S.
1998	Halfpipe	Rob Kingwill, U.S.	Terje Haakonsen, Norway	Todd Richards, U.S.
1997	Halfpipe	Todd Richards, U.S.	Terje Haakonsen, Norway	Sebu Kuhlberg, Finland
1996	Halfpipe	Jimi Scott, U.S.	Sami Hyry, Finland	Max Ploetzender, Austria
1995	Halfpipe	Terje Haakonsen, Norway	Jason Evans, U.S.	J.J. Collier, U.S.
1994	Halfpipe	Todd Richards, U.S.	Lael Gregory, U.S.	Jason Evans, U.S.
1993	Halfpipe	Terje Haakonsen, Norway	Keith Wallace, U.S.	Sebu Kuhlberg, Finland
1992	Halfpipe	Terje Haakonsen, Norway	Jeff Brushie, U.S.	Todd Richards, U.S.
1991	Halfpipe	Jimi Scott, U.S.	Craig Kelly, U.S.	Shaun Palmer, U.S.
1990	Halfpipe	Craig Kelly, U.S.	Shaun Palmer, U.S.	Jeff Brushie, U.S.
1989	Halfpipe	Craig Kelly, U.S.	Bert LaMar, U.S.	Terry Kidwell, U.S.
1988	Halfpipe	Terry Kidwell, U.S.	Bert LaMar, U.S.	Craig Kelly, U.S.
2006	Quarterpipe	Danny Davis, U.S.	Risto Matilla, Finland	Kevin Pearce, U.S.
2005	Rail Jam	Eddie Wall, U.S.	Yale Cousino, U.S.	Jed Anderson, U.S.
2004	Rail Jam	Rahm Klampert, U.S.	Travis Rice, U.S.	Chris Rotax, U.S.
2003	Rail Jam	Travis Rice, U.S.	Shaun White, U.S.	Zach Leach, U.S.
2006	Slopestyle	Shaun White, U.S.	Chas Guidemond, U.S.	Jussi Oksanen, Finland
2005	Slopestyle	Risto Matilla, Finland	Jussi Oksanen, Finland	Andreas Wiig, Norway
2004	Slopestyle	Jake Blauvelt, U.S.	Travis Rice, U.S.	Christopher Schmidt, Germany
2003	Slopestyle	Shaun White, U.S.	Travis Rice, U.S.	Nate Sheehan, U.S.
2002	Slopestyle	Rahm Klampert, U.S.	Travis Rice, U.S.	Ryan Paris, U.S.

WOMEN

YEAR	EVENT	GOLD	SILVER	BRONZE
2006	Halfpipe	Torah Bright, Australia	Gretchen Bleiler, U.S.	Elena Hight, U.S.
2005	Halfpipe	Gretchen Bleiler, U.S.	Torah Bright, Australia	Hannah Teter, U.S.
2004	Halfpipe	Kelly Clark, U.S.	Tricia Byrnes, U.S.	Stine Brun Kjeldaas, Norway
2003	Halfpipe	Gretchen Bleiler, U.S.	Natasza Zurek, Canada	Hannah Teter, U.S.
2002	Halfpipe	Kelly Clark, U.S.	Tricia Byrnes, U.S.	Stine Brun Kjeldaas, Norway
2001	Halfpipe	Natasza Zurek, Canada	Shannon Dunn, U.S.	Gretchen Bleiler, U.S.
2000	Halfpipe	Natasza Zurek, Canada	Shannon Dunn, U.S.	Barrett Christy, U.S.
1999	Halfpipe	Nicola Thost, Germany	Tricia Byrnes, U.S.	Shannon Dunn, U.S.
1998	Halfpipe	Nicola Thost, Germany	Tricia Byrnes, U.S.	Tara Teigen, Canada
1997	Halfpipe	Barrett Christy, U.S.	Tricia Byrnes, U.S.	Michelle Taggart, U.S.
1996	Halfpipe	Satu Jarvela, Finland	Michelle Taggart, U.S.	Jennie Waara, Sweden
1995	Halfpipe	Satu Jarvela, Finland	Nicole Angelrath, Switzerland	Jennie Waara, Sweden
1994	Halfpipe	Shannon Dunn, U.S	Tina Basich, U.S.	Sandra Farmand, Germany
1993	Halfpipe	Shannon Dunn, U.S.	Janna Meyen, U.S.	Tricia Byrnes, U.S.
1992	Halfpipe	Tricia Byrnes, U.S.	Nicole Angelrath, Switzerland	Tina Basich, U.S.
1991	Halfpipe	Janna Meyen, U.S.	Tina Basich, U.S.	Michelle Taggart, U.S.
1990	Halfpipe	Tina Basich, U.S.	Lisa Vinciguerra, U.S.	Jean Higgins, U.S.
1989	Halfpipe	Jean Higgins, U.S.	Tara Eberhard, U.S.	Ashild Lofthus, Norway
1988	Halfpipe	Petra Mussig, Germany	Jean Higgins, U.S.	Gayle Guerin, U.S.
2006	Quarterpipe	Hana Beaman, U.S.	Junko Asazuma, Japan	Molly Aguirre, U.S.
2005	Rail Jam	Leanne Pelosi, Canada	Hana Beaman, U.S.	Spencer O'Brien, Canada
2004	Rail Jam	Leanne Pelosi, Canada	Erin Comstock, U.S.	Natasza Zurek, Canada
2006	Slopestyle	Hana Beaman, U.S.	Spencer O'Brien, Canada	Jaime Anderson, U.S.
2005	Slopestyle	Janna Meyen, U.S.	Leanne Pelosi, Canada	Natasza Zurek, Canada
2004	Slopestyle	Priscilla Levac, Canada	Kelly Clark, U.S.	Hana Beaman, U.S.
2003	Slopestyle	Hana Beaman, U.S.	Priscilla Levac, Canada	Hannah Teter, U.S.
2002	Slopestyle	Annie Boulanger, Canada	Hannah Teter, U.S.	Jaime MacLeod, U.S.

WINTER OLYMPICS

MEN

YEAR	EVENT	GOLD	SILVER	BRONZE
2006	Giant Slalom	Philipp Schoch, Switzerland	Simon Schoch, Switzerland	Siegfried Grabner, Austria
2002	Giant Slalom	Philipp Schoch, Switzerland	Richard Richardsson, Sweden	Chris Klug, U.S.
1998	Giant Slalom	Ross Rebagliati, Canada	Thomas Prugger, Italy	Ueli Kestenholz, Switzerland
2006	Halfpipe	Shaun White, U.S.	Danny Kass, U.S.	Markku Koski, Finland
2002	Halfpipe	Ross Powers, U.S.	Danny Kass, U.S.	Jarret Thomas, U.S.
1998	Halfpipe	Gian Simmen, Switzerland	Daniel Franck, Norway	Ross Powers, U.S.
2006	Snowboardcross	Seth Wescott, U.S.	Radoslav Zidek, Slovakia	Paul-Henri Delerue, France

WOMEN

YEAR	EVENT	GOLD	SILVER	BRONZE
2006	Giant Slalom	Daniela Meuli, Switzerland	Amelie Kober, Germany	Rosey Fletcher, U.S.
2002	Giant Slalom	Isabelle Blanc, France	Karine Ruby, France	Lidia Trettel, Italy
1998	Giant Slalom	Karine Ruby, France	Heidi Maria Renoth, Germany	Brigitte Koeck, Austria
2006	Halfpipe	Hanna Teeter, U.S.	Gretchen Bleiler, U.S.	Kjersti Buaas, Norway
2002	Halfpipe	Kelly Clark, U.S.	Doriane Vidal, France	Fabienne Reuteler, Switzerland
1998	Halfpipe	Nicola Thost, Germany	Stine Brun Kjeldaas, Norway	Shannon Dunn, U.S.
2006	Snowboardcross	Tanja Frieden, Switzerland	Lindsey Jacobellis, U.S.	Dominique Maltais, Canada

THE ARCTIC CHALLENGE

YEAR	EVENT	GOLD	SILVER	BRONZE
2005	Halfpipe	Not held due to weather	Not held due to weather	Not held due to weather
2004	Halfpipe	Andy Finch, U.S.	Steve Fisher, U.S.	Risto Mattila, Finland
2003	Halfpipe (Best Run)	Shaun White, U.S.	Not awarded	Not awarded
	Halfpipe (Highest Air)	Gian Simmen, Switzerland	Not awarded	Not awarded
	Halfpipe (Best Trick)	Marius Otterstad, Norway	Not awarded	Not awarded
	Halfpipe (Best Entry)	Halvor Lunn, Norway	Not awarded	Not awarded
2002	The Arctic Challenge canceled			
2001	Halfpipe	Shaun White, U.S.	Terje Haakonsen, Norway	Danny Kass, U.S.
2000	Halfpipe	Terje Haakonsen, Norway	Gian Simmen, Switzerland	Ingemar Backman, Sweden
1999	No judging this year			
2005	Slopestyle	Not held due to weather	Not held due to weather	Not held due to weather
2004	Slopestyle	Not held due to weather	Not held due to weather	Not held due to weather
2003	Slopestyle	Shaun White, U.S.	Heikki Sorsa, Finland	Nate Sheehan, U.S.

YEAR	EVENT	WINNER	YEAR	EVENT	WINNER
2005	Overall	Markus Keller, Switzerland	2005	Highest Air	Andy Finch, U.S.
2004	Overall	Travis Rice, U.S.	2004	Highest Air	Andy Finch, U.S.
2003	Overall	Travis Rice, U.S.	2003	Highest Air	Terje Haakonsen, Norway
2002	The Arctic Challenge canceled		2002	The Arctic Challenge canceled	
2001	Overall	Gian Simmen, Switzerland	2001	Highest Air	Heikki Sorsa, Finland
2000	Overall	Romain De Marchi, Switzerland	2000	Highest Air	Terje Haakonsen, Norway
1999	No judging this year		1999	No judging this year	
2005	Best Trick	Andy Finch, U.S.			
2004	Best Trick	Travis Rice, U.S.			
2003	Best Trick	Terje Haakonsen, Norway			
2002	The Arctic Challenge canceled				
2001	Best Trick	Gian Simmen, Switzerland			
2000	Best Trick	Romain De Marchi, Switzerland			
1999	No judging this year				

TOP 10 PLACES TO RIDE

1 **WHISTLER BLACKCOMB, BRITISH COLUMBIA, CANADA.** Whistler and Blackcomb mountains have 8,000 acres of terrain and the longest season in North America. With multiple parks and three pipes, Whistler Blackcomb has something for every level, plus insane backcountry and year-round rides on Palmer Glacier. The mountains are home to many pros and will host the snowboard events during the 2010 Olympic Games in nearby Vancouver.

Mammoth Mountain, California

2 **MAMMOTH MOUNTAIN, CALIFORNIA.** Pros such as Shaun White, Danny Kass, and Tara Dakides ride here because of the amazing variety of terrain. Mammoth has one of the best parks and pipes in the world, plus backcountry and a long season.

3 **BRECKENRIDGE, COLORADO.** The Superpipe sets Breckenridge apart from other Colorado resorts. The pipe hosts an annual Grand Prix event. Breck is home to the first snowboard park and top pros such as Chad Otterstrom and Todd Richards.

Breckenridge, Colorado

4 **LAKE TAHOE, CALIFORNIA/NEVADA.** Spanning two states, the Lake Tahoe area has the highest concentration of resorts (more than a dozen) in North America. Sierra-at-Tahoe has the best park, with obstacles for even the youngest ripper. The area has heavy backcountry terrain and gets credit for being the birthplace of snowboarding on the West Coast.

5 **PARK CITY/SALT LAKE CITY, UTAH.** This was the home of the 2002 Winter Olympics. Park City Mountain Resort has one of the finest terrain parks around, King's Crown Superpark. Many top pros go there to be photographed for snowboarding magazines. Eagle Superpipe, at 22 feet tall, is one of the biggest in the world and will host the World Championships in March 2006. Meanwhile, Salt Lake City natives and rail rulers JP Walker and Jeremy Jones practically invented street snowboarding on the local urban terrain.

6 TALMA, FINLAND. Talma is a small resort outside of Helsinki, Finland's capital. It has become the place for jib talent, such as Heikki Sorsa, and just about every other Finnish pro. Talma has a small hill, only 180 feet high, but the terrain is like the ultimate skatepark.

Talma, Finland

7 HEMSEDAL, NORWAY. Hemsedal has a halfpipe and two quarterpipes, which attract touring pros. But with three levels of park terrain, Hemsedal offers obstacles for novices, too.

8 SNOW PARK, NEW ZEALAND. Snow Park is a 60-acre playground of boxes, rainbow rails, C-rails, big kickers, superpipes, and jibs. The park is well maintained and has become a favorite haunt of top pros, who come to film and ride during the summer, when it's winter in the Southern Hemisphere.

Mt. Bachelor, Bend, Oregon

9 MT. BACHELOR, BEND, OREGON. Mt. Bachelor is located on an old volcano, and it blows away other resorts due to its lack of crowds and sunny springtime weather. It also has big backcountry terrain, plus one of the best parks (hips, rails, bars, and a fun box) and superpipes (home to an annual Grand Prix event).

10 MOUNT SNOW, VERMONT. Size and variety set Mount Snow apart from other East Coast resorts. It has four terrain parks and a superpipe that cover 40 acres. Mount Snow had the first terrain park in the East. The resort hosted the Winter X Games in 2000 and 2001 and is home to Winter Olympic gold medalist Kelly Clark.

CHAPTER 7

SNOWMOBILING

Huge air and backflips on a 400-pound motorized monster? Why not? These action sports athletes are just getting warmed up.

Blair Morgan has ruled the race courses for 10 seasons.

JASON GILMOUR

For centuries, people have struggled to travel through deep snow. The native inhabitants of North America used snowshoes and dogsleds. Northern Europeans invented skis. In modern times, man has used machines.

One of these men was Carl Eliason of Sayner, Wisconsin. In 1924, Eliason invented the first snowmobile. Using skis, a 2.5-horsepower outboard motor, and bicycle parts, he created a vehicle that could carry two people. He called it a motor toboggan.

Others had already created machines for off-road snow travel. One was an automobile that had the front wheels replaced with skis for steering and the back wheels with a track to push the car through the snow. A track is a belt found on heavy construction equipment. Because it is longer than a wheel, the track distributes the vehicle's weight over a larger area and prevents it from sinking.)

Eliason's idea was new. He adapted the track system to create a small, personal snowmobile. Plus, he added wooden cleats to the track for better traction.

Over the next 15 years, Eliason manufactured his motor toboggan in small quantities. By the 1940's, he had joined forces with an automobile company to mass-produce the vehicle. During World War II, the United States Army bought 150 of them for use in Alaska.

Everyone into the Snow

By the 1950's, other manufacturers had begun mass-producing snowmobiles. Polaris Industries, of Roseau, Minnesota, got into the business in 1955. In 1959, Bombardier, a motor company based in Valcourt, Quebec, Canada, introduced the Ski-Doo.

The Ski-Doo would become the standard for modern snowmobiles. It used a small engine and had lightweight parts. As a result, it was sleeker and better-looking than the others on the market.

The timing was excellent for mass-produced snowmobiles. The United States and Canada were prospering, and their citizens were looking for fun ways to spend their newfound time and money. Although popular with hunters, trappers, and prospectors, the Ski-Doo

MARCUS PAULSEN/SHAZAMM/ESPN IMAGES

Tucker Hibbert is a pro motorcross racer as well as a top snowmobiler.

also became a huge hit with outdoors enthusiasts.

Manufacturers competed to show whose snowmobile was best. Some staged long journeys to demonstrate their machines' performance. In March 1960, Polaris founder Edgar Hetteen and three companions snowmobiled from Bethel, Alaska, to Fairbanks, Alaska. The journey, across 1,200 miles and through subzero temperatures, wind storms, and deep snow, took 21 days.

In 1968, Ralph Plaisted of St. Paul, Minnesota, led a Ski-Doo crew 825 miles in 43 days over the frozen Arctic to reach the North Pole — the first expedition to reach the top of the globe by land.

In 1961, Hetteen left Polaris to start Arctic Cat. In 1968, motorcycle manufacturer Yamaha began making snowmobiles. Soon, hundreds of companies were in the business, and sales were booming.

Jay Quinlan was one of the pioneers of freestyle snowmobiling.

The Races Are On

Competition among manufacturers led to competition among snowmobilers. The sport's first organized event, the Canadian Power Toboggan Championships, was held in 1963 in Beausejour, Manitoba, Canada. The first race in the United States was run in 1964 in Eagle River, Wisconsin. The winner was a 13-year-old named Stan Hayes.

The United States Snowmobile Association (USSA), was founded in 1965, and began organizing races two years later. The biggest events were oval racing, where riders raced laps around an icy track; cross-country; drag racing (called snodrags); and hill climbing (or hillcross).

However, during the 1980's, a new type of racing developed at a ski resort in Quadna, Minnesota. It was called snocross. Snocross took cross-country racing and put it on a smaller course full of bumps and jumps. It was a lot like motocross on snow.

Turning Up the Action

Early snocross competitions were tame by today's standards. But that would change in 1992 with the start of the Duluth (Minnesota) National Snocross competiton.

The race's founders had been inspired by the aggressive style and aerial maneuvers of Scandinavian racers. One of those, Toni Haikonen of Finland, arrived to compete at the Duluth National and other races in North America. The "Flying Finn" stunned the crowds by launching over two and three jumps at a time.

Now the only thing holding back the sport was equipment. Manufacturers responded by improving the system of shocks and supports that softens landings on bumpy terrain. The new and improved sleds led to more exciting aerial riding, which helped snocross grow in popularity. In 1998, it was added to the Winter X Games. Haikonen won the first gold medal.

Snowmobiling continued to evolve into an action sport. A motocross racer from Canada named Blair Morgan adapted the stand-up racing style of motorcycles to snowmobiles. From 1997 through 2006, he would win 11 national snocross season titles (in both the Pro Open and Pro Stock divisions) and seven Winter X Games medals.

Meanwhile, aerial snowmobile riding was growing out West, especially in the mountainous backcountry of Alaska. Here, riders launched off natural and man-made jumps, pulling BMX and freestyle motocross tricks.

The difficulty level of freestyle tricks progressed quickly. In 2001, Jim Rippey pulled the first recorded backflip on a snowmobile.

Fast and exciting, both freestyle and snocross are the future of snowmobile competition. They have brought the sport from cold weather climates to the rest of the world.

FAST FACT
Snocross tracks range in length from three-eighths to three-fourths of a mile. Races usually run from 10 to 20 laps.

< U P – A N D – C O M E R >
STEVE MARTIN

Only 21 years old, Steve Martin is already a veteran of elite snowmobile racing competition. He is one of the smaller riders, at 5' 5" tall, but has surprising strength and handles his sled with great skill. Martin emerged as a top racer while still a teenager, winning silver and bronze at the Winter X Games in Hillcross, an event that has since been dropped. In 2004, Martin suffered a serious setback when he broke his back during practice at the Games. Healthy again in 2005, he returned better than ever, winning the World Snowmobile Association Snocross Pro Open points championship and a bronze medal in Snocross at the Winter X Games. Expect Martin to dominate snocross in coming years.

JASON GILMOUR

INNOVATOR
JOSEPH-ARMAND BOMBARDIER

Joseph-Armand Bombardier was born in 1907 in the small town of Valcourt, Quebec, Canada. He had a passion for building things, and became a mechanic when he grew up. In 1934, his son died from an illness after deep snows prevented him from reaching a hospital. The tragedy inspired Bombardier to build a machine that could travel in the worst winter conditions. In 1935, he developed a wheel and track with a rubber covering that provided excellent traction in snow. Bombardier started a company to build vehicles that could carry up to seven people. In 1959, his company developed the Ski-Doo, a snowmobile with wooden skis that could travel up to 25 miles per hour. Although not the first small snowmobile, the Ski-Doo featured a rubber track, lighter engine, and simple clutch for changing gears. It opened up the world of snowmobiling to anyone who just loved to be outdoors.

Bombardier and his early model snowmobile.

MUSÉE J. ARMAND BOMBARDIER (2)

BACKFLIP

FRED FOTO

JIM RIPPEY

Jim Rippey was already a successful pro snowboarder when he turne the new sport of freestyle snowmobiling upside down in 2001. Durir the filming of the freestyle snowmobile video *Slednecks 4*, he mac history by becoming the first person to land a backflip on a sle Rippey was an experienced rider; he used snowmobiles to cruise tl backcountry looking for fresh snowboard spots. But he had nev tried a flip before. He set up for his stunt on a mountainside in t backcountry outside Dry Fork, Utah. Rippey launched off a kicker jump ramp that directs the rider up, rather than out) on his 400-pou snowmobile four times and bailed each time. On his fifth try, he soar 20 feet through the air, flipped and nailed the landing. The footage Rippey's flip was a landmark in snowmobiling. A flip was a li threatening stunt, and others had been seriously injured trying it. Fi years later, the backflip is still considered one of the most diffic and dangerous tricks in freestyle snowmobiling.

TIME LINE

1924 Carl Eliason, of Sayner, Wisconsin, builds a motorized toboggan in his spare time, using skis and a 2.5 horsepower outboard motor.

The Father of Invention

1942 Joseph-Armand Bombardier opens a factory in Montreal, Quebec, Canada, to mass-produce large snowmobiles for the Canadian military.

1955 A new company, Polaris Industries of Minnesota, begins making snowmobile prototypes.

1959 Bombard unveils t Ski-Doo, the first mas produced recreational snowmobile. Its desig will be the standard fo future models.

118 SNOWMOBILING

NECESSARY OBJECTS

- **SNOWMOBILE:** There are three main types of recreational snowmobiles: mountain, trail, and high performance. They all have the same major components:
  a. The track, usually a rough rubber, pushes the sled through the snow. Tracks come in different lengths and widths for different terrain.
  b. The engine pushes the track. The smallest engine is a 370cc two-stroke model. (The term *cc* stands for cubic centimeters and refers to the size of an engine's chambers. The larger the chambers, the more powerful the engine. Engines can be two-stroke or four-stroke. As a general rule, two-stroke engines are more powerful than four-stroke engines with the same sized chambers). The most common snowmobile engine is a 500cc two-stroke. In recent years more manufacturers have begun to turn to four-stroke engines, which are more fuel-efficient, quieter, and less polluting.
  c. The suspension helps reduce the impact from bumps and jumps. The type of suspension depends on the weight of the rider and the terrain that will be ridden.
  d. The skis slide along the snow, helping steer the sled. Just as in Alpine skiing, a trend has been to use skis with a greater sidecut, which allows for tighter turns.

- **SNOWMOBILE SUIT/GLOVES:** The best snowmobile clothing keeps cold out. Snowmobile dealers sell jackets and pants specifically for this purpose, but gear found in outdoor sports stores can also do the trick. Make sure to dress in layers, with a protective outer shell that keeps out cold air and moisture. Clothes should be formfitting. Never wear a scarf, which can catch on trees and other objects. Get snowmobiling gloves with fingers. Mittens make it difficult to operate the throttle and brake.

- **BOOTS:** Snowmobile boots tend to be big, heavy, and ugly. Buy them from a snowmobile dealership or an outdoors store. Warm and dry feet make for happy riding.

- **HELMET:** Snowmobile helmets are similar in appearance to motorcycle helmets, but are better insulated. Buy from a snowmobile dealer and be sure the helmet is certified for safety by the Department of Transportation. To prevent frostbite, make sure the helmet comes with a chin guard and full face shield. Many riders wear a balaclava, a head covering with eye and mouth holes, under their helmet to keep warm.

FAST FACT

The Ski-Doo, which debuted as the first recreational snowmobile in 1959, was originally called the Ski-Dog. However, because of a typographical error, the *g* wound up being changed to an *o*.

1961 Arctic Cat is founded in Minnesota.

A New Breed

1963 The longest-running snowmobile event, the Canadian Power Toboggan Championships, holds its first race in Beausejour, Manitoba, Canada.

1964 The first snowmobile race in the United States is held on an oval racetrack in Eagle River, Wisconsin. It later becomes the Eagle River World Championship.

1967 The Sno Barons Snowmobile Club of Minnesota, debuts Hay Days, a fall festival with snowmobiling drag racing on grass. The United States Snowmobile Association begins sanctioning snowmobile races.

THE BASIC TRICKS

CANCAN▶

This trick is named after a lively French dance in which you kick your legs high in the air. Cancans are a basic-to-intermediate trick. First, launch your snowmobile in the air. Then, kick one leg over the top of the seat to the other side before returning it to the foot boards. When you're comfortable performing the kicks with your right and left feet, graduate to the two-footed cancan and kick both feet to the same side of the sled.

JASON GILMOUR

JASON GILMOUR

◀NO-HANDED AII

A no-hander is tougher than a no-footed air, because you have to let g of the handlebars for a second — a scary thing for novices. Try one-handed airs first to get the feel. Alternate with one hand and then the other, before busting loose and letting both hands free. Remember ▮ grab the bars again before touching down — no-handed landings are a more advanced move.

┣TIME LINE┣

1968
Motorcycle manufacturer Yamaha enters the snowmobile market.

1972 Mike Trapp wins the World's Championship at Eagle River for the second straight year, becoming the first to win consecutive titles in the event.

1974 Stan Hayes, who won the first World's Championship at Eagle River in 1964 at age 13, is named the first Sno Pro Driver of the Year.

Stan Hayes

COURTESY OF C.J. RAMSTAD

1985 The Internatio Snowmobile Hall of Fa and Museum is founde in Eagle River, Wisconsi It is currently being moved to St. Germain, Wisconsin.

SELKO PHOTO

SUPERMAN▲

This is an intermediate-to-advanced trick on a snowmobile. When done properly, the rider looks like Superman flying through the air. First, you have to get air by launching off a jump. Once in the air, keep hold of the handlebars and fully extend your arms and legs (feet together) as far back as possible. (Your body should be nearly parallel to the ground.) Next, quickly return your feet to the boards and prepare to land. After mastering the basic Superman, you can try advanced variations, such as one-handed grabs and seat grabs — where you hold onto the seat instead of the handlebars.

F🅐S🆃 FACT

There are approximately 2.6 million registered snowmobiles in the world, according to the International Snowmobile Manufacturer's Association. Of those, about 1.75 million are in the United States.

992
e annual
Juluth National
nocross race
started in
innesota.

1998 The Winter X Games adds its first snowmobile event, Snocross. Toni Haikonen wins gold.

1999 The first *Slednecks* video debuts, showing snowmobiles roaring off jumps and riders pulling tricks. The images help launch a freestyle craze.

2001 Jim Rippey lands the first recorded backflip on a snowmobile in Dry Forks, Utah.

2006 Blair Morgan wins his record fifth Winter X Games gold medal in Snocross.

Blair Morgan

ALLEN KEE/WIREIMAGE.COM

< LEGEND >
BLAIR MORGAN

Blair Morgan has been so dominant in his sport's early years that the snocross record book could be titled, *The Blair Morgan Story.* During the past 10 years, Morgan has won half of all national races, including 11 championships and seven medals at the Winter X Games. Morgan intimidates other racers with his confidence and aggressive style on the track, and his brash talk off of it. He pioneered a standing style while riding, similar to that used in motocross. Other riders have copied Morgan's style, but no one has been able to match his record. Now 30, Morgan has been slowed by injuries the past three years. Still, he is capable of winning any given race, which he proved again at the 2006 Winter X Games, collecting his record fifth gold medal.

< GREATEST MOMENT >
SNOCROSS DEBUTS AT THE WINTER X GAMES

Snocross grew quickly from its start in Minnesota in the mid-1980's to become the most popular form of snowmobile racing. Toni Haikonen of Finland helped snocross develop by introducing an exciting aerial style. Fans flocked to the races, and the track's small size allowed spectators to easily see all the action. However, snocross requires cold and snow, and was mostly unknown outside of Canada and the northern United States. Then, in 1998, snocross made its debut on national television at the Winter X Games. There, Haikonen put on an air show. He soared 30 feet over jumps and won the gold medal. Afterward, interest in snocross spiked: The World Snowmobile Association (WSA) has grown from 800 riders in 1998 to more than 3,000 today. (The WSA has joined another organization and will now be known as the World PowerSports Association, or WPSA.)

TOP 10 ATHLETES

1 **BLAIR MORGAN**, born October 9, 1975, in Prince Albert, Saskatchewan, Canada. Morgan is known as Superman by his peers for the way he dominates snocross. He has won half the national races and 12 championships in the past 10 years. He has dominated at the Winter X Games, winning seven medals, including five golds. In the summer, Morgan races pro motocross.

2 **TUCKER HIBBERT**, born June 24, 1984, in Driggs, Idaho. At age 15, Hibbert shocked veteran riders in 2000 when he won Snocross gold at the Winter X Games. During the next three years, he won three WSA points championships. At 18, he retired from full-time snocross competition to pursue pro motocross racing, but still competes at the X Games each year.

3 **STEVE MARTIN**, born June 23, 1984, in Evanston, Wyoming. The most promising young rider around, the 21-year-old Martin broke out in 2005: He won bronze in Snocross at the Winter X Games and finished first in the WSA Pro Open points race.

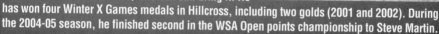

Carl Kuster

4 **CARL KUSTER**, born December 18, 1975, in Westlock, Alberta, Canada. Kuster is a veteran hillcross and snocross racer, who can still bring it. He has won four Winter X Games medals in Hillcross, including two golds (2001 and 2002). During the 2004-05 season, he finished second in the WSA Open points championship to Steve Martin.

5 **T.J. GULLA**, born March 20, 1981, in South Hero, Vermont. Gulla has won two medals at the Winter X Games: gold in Hillcross (2003) and bronze in Snocross (2000). His best season on the WSA circuit came in 2004-05 when he won the Pro Stock points title.

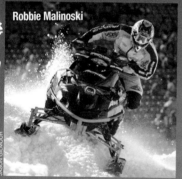

Robbie Malinoski

6 **D.J. ECKSTROM**, born November 9, 1980, in Duluth, Minnesota. A veteran in snocross, Eckstrom is one of the most consistent riders. He has won bronze (2001) and silver (2003) medals at the Winter X Games.

7 **MIKE ISLAND**, born June 14, 1981, in Warminster, Ontario, Canada. Island won Winter X Games gold in Snocross in 2004. He is a hard-charging competitor, but has struggled to keep his aggression in check.

8 **ROBBIE MALINOSKI**, born September 30, 1981, in Humboldt, Saskatchewan, Canada. In 2003 Malinoski was named WSA Most Improved Driver of the Year. In 2004-05 he finished third in the WSA Pro Stock points championship.

9 **CHRIS BURANDT**, born October 14, 1978, in Denver, Colorado. An all-around talent on a sled, Burandt has gained fame for his freeriding backcountry moves in the *Slednecks* video series. In competition, he won the Red Bull Fuel and Fury event in 2005. He was runner-up in the International Freestyle Snocross Association points standings in 2004.

10 **JAY QUINLAN**, born April 27, 1979, in Valdez, Alaska. Quinlan was the first to pull a backflip in competition, at the 2003 Red Bull Fuel and Fury event. He also won the 2000 Winter Gravity Games freestyle event. He started out competing in professional snocross.

WINTER X GAMES RESULTS

YEAR	EVENT	GOLD	SILVER	BRONZE
2006	Snocross	Blair Morgan, Canada	Levi LaVallee, U.S.	Ross Martin, U.S.
2005	Snocross	Blair Morgan, Canada	Tucker Hibbert, U.S.	Steven Martin, U.S.
2004	Snocross	Michael Island, Canada	Tucker Hibbert, U.S.	Blair Morgan, Canada
2003	Snocross	Blair Morgan, Canada	D.J. Eckstrom, U.S.	Tucker Hibbert, U.S.
2002	Snocross	Blair Morgan, Canada	Tucker Hibbert, U.S.	Tomi Ahmasalo, Finland
2001	Snocross	Blair Morgan, Canada	Kent Ipsen, U.S.	D.J. Eckstrom, U.S.
2000	Snocross	Tucker Hibbert, U.S.	Blair Morgan, Canada	T.J. Gulla, U.S.
1999	Snocross	Chris Vincent, U.S.	Blair Morgan, Canada	Trevor John, U.S.
1998	Snocross	Tony Haikonen, Finland	Dennis Burks, U.S.	Per Berggren, Sweden
2004	Hillcross	Levi LaVallee, U.S.	Justin Tate, U.S.	Carl Kuster, Canada
2003	Hillcross	T.J. Gulla, U.S.	Carl Kuster, Canada	Steve Martin, Canada
2002	Hillcross	Carl Kuster, Canada	Steve Martin, Canada	Rick Ward, U.S.
2001	Hillcross	Carl Kuster, Canada	Vinny Clark, Canada	Matt Luczynski, U.S.

WORLD SNOWMOBILING ASSOCIATION PRO OPEN RESULTS

YEAR	EVENT	GOLD	SILVER	BRONZE
2004-05	Snocross	Steve Martin, U.S.	Carl Kuster, Canada	D.J. Eckstrom, U.S.
2003-04	Snocross	Blair Morgan, Canada	Michael Island, Canada	D.J. Eckstrom, U.S.
2002-03	Snocross	Blair Morgan, Canada	Tucker Hibbert, U.S.	Carl Kuster, Canada
2001-02	Snocross	Tucker Hibbert, U.S.	Blair Morgan, Canada	D.J. Eckstrom, U.S.
2000-01	Snocross	Tucker Hibbert, U.S.	Blair Morgan, Canada	D.J. Eckstrom, U.S.
1999-00	Snocross	Blair Morgan, Canada	D.J. Eckstrom, U.S.	Kent Ipsen, U.S.

FSX FREESTYLE SNOWCROSS RESULTS

YEAR	EVENT	GOLD	SILVER	BRONZE
2004-05	Freestyle	Lee Stuart, Canada	Ryan Britt, U.S.	Jimmy Flood, U.S.
2003-04	Freestyle	Heath Frisby, U.S.	Chris Burandt, U.S.	Lee Stuart, Canada

RED BULL FUEL AND FURY RESULTS

YEAR	EVENT	GOLD	SILVER	BRONZE
2005	Freestyle	Chris Burandt, U.S.	Justin Hoyer, U.S.	Heath Frisby, U.S.
2004	Freestyle	Justin Hoyer, U.S.	Lee Stuart, Canada	Chris Burandt, U.S.
2003	Freestyle	Jay Quinlan, U.S.	Heath Frisby, U.S.	Ryan Britt, U.S.

TOP 10 PLACES TO RIDE

1 PARK X, HILL CITY, MINNESOTA. Located on the grounds of the Quadna Mountain Resort, Park X is a one-of-a-kind facility for snowmobile racing and training. Track builders use snow-making equipment to shape bumps and berms into a naturally hilly terrain. The pros on the WPSA snowmobile tour rate it their favorite race site.

2 WEST YELLOWSTONE, MONTANA. West Yellowstone is famous for its heavy snowfalls and hundreds of miles of trails. The area offers everything from mellow rides along groomed trails to big drops into deep powder.

3 HAY DAYS, FOREST LAKE, MINNESOTA. Sno Barons snowmobile club has proven that snowmobiles don't actually require snow. Since 1967, the Barons have hosted the annual Hay Days festival, which kicks off the snowmobile season in September. The largest event in snowmobiling, it offers a weird twist: snowmobile drag racing on grass.

Revelstoke

KIP WILEY

4 MCCALL, IDAHO. McCall lies in a stunning valley at 5,000 feet above sea level, where each winter heavy snows fall. With 500 miles of groomed trails, plus some serious mountain powder, McCall is a cool place to ride.

5 REVELSTOKE, BRITISH COLUMBIA, CANADA. Located between the Monashee and Selkirk Mountain ranges of Western Canada, Revelstoke receives an average of 60 feet of snow each winter — a season that lasts almost the whole year. With beautiful scenery and miles of open spaces to explore, the area is a magnet for serious snowmobilers.

6 CABLE, WISCONSIN. Hundreds of miles of groomed wilderness trails, plus places to stop, rest, and eat along the way, make Cable an ideal launching point. Rides through the Chequamegon National Forest offer glimpses of wildlife and the natural landscape.

7 KEWEENAW PENINSULA, MICHIGAN. Surrounded on three sides by Lake Superior, the Keweenaw Peninsula has 200 miles of trails, which connect to more than 2,000 more miles in Michigan's Upper Peninsula. All of which means days of trail riding through the wilderness.

Keweenaw

KEWEENAW TOURISM COUNCIL

8 JACKSON HOLE, WYOMING. More than 6,000 feet up in the Teton Range, the Jackson area provides some spectacular views. Opportunities for extreme mountain riding abound. Jackson hosts the biggest event in hillclimbing, the annual World Championship Snowmobile Hill Climb.

9 ALASKA. Alaska's motto should be Go Wild because it offers the only true wilderness frontier left in the United States. There are few groomed trails in the state, but millions of acres of backcountry riding. With heavy snows and a long season, Alaska offers unlimited opportunities to explore.

10 LAKE GENEVA, WISCONSIN. The final site of the World Snowmobile Association/World PowerSports Association pro tour is also one of the most popular with pro riders. The course, on the grounds of the Grand Geneva Resort, features big hills and hairy drops.

CHAPTER 8

SURFING

The sport has come a long way since the 1700's, when natives of the South Pacific rode waves on wooden planks.

Hawaiian-born Andy Irons is a three-time world champion.

ASPWORLDTOUR.COM/TOSTEE

The first written record of surfing dates back to 1779. British sea captain James Cook and his crew became the first Europeans to sail to the Hawaiian Islands. Describing their journey, a member of Cook's crew wrote about natives riding waves on wooden boards. At the time, everyone in Hawaii, from chiefs to common people, surfed. But that would soon change.

During the next 100 years, surfing — and Hawaiians — suffered. Diseases brought over by the Europeans killed thousands of the islands' people. Newly arrived Christian missionaries said surfing was immoral and discouraged it.

The sport might have died out altogether if not for a group of hard-core surfers at Waikiki Beach, near Honolulu, now the Hawaiian capital. As the city grew during the early 1900's, the surfers at Waikiki inspired visitors and residents alike to take up the sport.

Sofia Mulanovich is the first South American to win the ASP world championship.

Showing the World

Among the Waikiki group was a superb surfer and swimmer named Duke Kahanamoku. He became an international celebrity after he won the gold medal in 100-meter freestyle swimming at the 1912 Olympics. He traveled the world, giving swimming demonstrations in places like California, New Jersey, and Australia. But if the waves were good, he also showed off his surfing skills. For the next 50 years, Kahanamoku was the ambassador for surfing — and Hawaii. (He would also compete in the 1920 and 1924 Olympics, winning gold medals in the 100-meter freestyle and 4 x 200-meter freestyle relay in 1920 and a silver medal in the 100-meter freestyle in 1924.)

As a result of the efforts of Kahanamoku and others, dedicated surfing communities grew in Southern California, Australia, and Hawaii. But surfboard design limited the sport's growth. At the time, boards were either 10-foot-long wooden slabs that weighed more than 100 pounds or 16-foot rafts that were long and hollow. In the 1950's, the introduction of fiberglass and resins allowed manufacturers to make boards that were smaller, faster, and easier to control. These boards let surfers carve turns and challenge bigger waves.

The Foam Board

Another huge step forward for surfing took place in 1958, when Hobie Alter and Gordon "Grubby" Clark created the first polyurethane foam boards. Foam was cheap, easy to shape, and allowed for mass

Layne Beachley
holds the record for
most world titles
for a woman (six).

production of surfboards for the first time. Demand for surfboards grew quickly following the 1959 release of *Gidget*, a movie about a girl from Malibu, California, and her surfer friends. The carefree lifestyle shown on screen inspired lots of viewers to catch a wave.

The Growing Surf Scene

Surfing continued to increase in popularity throughout the 1960's. Surf scenes popped up in California, Australia, Hawaii, South Africa, and parts of the East Coast of the United States.

Despite the high skill level of top surfers, the sport was still mostly an amateur pastime. Only a few professional tournaments existed in the 1960's and early 1970's. A group of Australians held the first

modern professional competition in 1961. George Smith won the contest — and $2. But by 1976, pro surfing contests in far-flung parts of the globe were organized into a series that would become today's Association of Surfing Professionals (ASP).

FAST FACT

Laird Hamilton has worked as a stuntman in surfing scenes on the movies *Waterworld* (1995) and *Die Another Day* (2002).

Peter Townend of Australia won the first world championship that year. The Australians would dominate pro surfing for the next 10 years. Aussie Mark Richards won four titles from 1979 to 1982. By the mid-1980's, Tom Curren of the United States reigned as world champ, and others tried to copy his powerful, flowing style.

Surfing's New Style

In the 1990's, a teenage superstar from Florida named Kelly Slater arrived on the pro scene. He introduced a new style of riding that was influenced by skateboarding tricks. Slater slashed across waves like no one had before. He pulled more moves per wave, but was always in control on the moving water.

For almost 10 years, Slater was untouchable, winning six world titles between 1992 and 1998. Though still in his prime, he retired in 1999, then returned to the sport in 2002. In 2005, he won a seventh world championship.

Today's pro events are held where the world's best waves are. These locations are known as breaks. Pro superstars can make millions of dollars from contest winnings and endorsements. Meanwhile, other types of surfing have evolved: Big-wave riding has moved into areas that were once thought to be unrideable. Surfers such as Laird Hamilton are towed out by personal watercraft to fast-moving waves at offshore reefs. Once there, they attempt to conquer 30-foot-plus beasts.

But it's not just the best and most challenging breaks that are being tested these days. Die-hard surfers can be found just about anywhere there are waves.

INNOVATOR
LAIRD HAMILTON

TOM SERVAIS/A-FRAME

Surfers of the 1900's were "watermen," experts at swimming, diving, fishing, kayaking, and interpreting weather. Laird Hamilton is the modern-day link to these legendary figures. His surf-legend stepfather, Billy Hamilton, raised him on the Hawaiian islands of Oahu and Kauai. At 6' 3" and 215 pounds, Hamilton has unmatched skills as a surfer, swimmer, windsurfer, and kayaker. He is not just a throwback to another era, however. Hamilton has been surfing's future, leading the sport into uncharted waters. (At right, he rides a foilboard, which lets him move through the water with less resistance than a regular surfboard.)

Some waves along Hawaii's outer reefs were considered unrideable because of their size and speed. No surfer could paddle fast enough to catch one. During the 1980's, Hamilton and a friend experimented with being towed into big waves using a small boat. In 1992, they set their sights on a spot called "Jaws," a half-mile off the coast of Maui. The surfers were towed by personal watercraft into monster waves that were 40 to 70 feet high — and rode them. Hamilton's pioneering tow-in rides brought attention to big-wave surfing.

< LEGEND >
LISA ANDERSEN

The Ormond Beach, Florida, native was the only girl surfing in her hometown when she took up the sport at age 13. Surfing was her escape from a troubled home life. Lisa Andersen's parents didn't approve of her surfing and often grounded her for riding waves. At age 16, she ran away to Huntington Beach, California, to become a pro. She slept on friends' couches, surfed every day, and waited tables for money. Riding with male surfers helped Andersen develop a powerful style. She won the U.S. championships in 1987. She turned pro the following year and was named rookie of the year. Still, Andersen lacked consistency in contests and didn't win her first world title until 1994. Then she won the next three (1995-97) before retiring midway through the 1998 season due to back problems. Andersen's dominance, attitude, and beauty made her a women's surfing icon. She showed women that they could ride a surfboard as well as a man and still be feminine.

ASPWORLDTOUR.COM/TOSTEE

< UP–AND–COMER >
CARISSA MOORE

Although she's just 13 years old, Carissa Moore has been making waves in women's surfing for several years. At age 11, the little ripper from Honolulu, Hawaii, made the finals of a pro contest, the Body Glove Surfbout. She was the youngest surfer to reach the finals of an ASP event. She is also the only surfer to win three divisions (Open Women, Explorer Women, and Middle School Girls) at the National Scholastic Surfing Association National Championships, in 2003. At her current rate of conquest, Moore will be the best in the world — at any age — before she graduates from high school.

ASPWORLDTOUR.COM/KAREN

NECESSARY
OBJECTS

● **WET SUIT:** A regular bathing suit works fine for surfing in warm water. But as surfing spread to cold-water places such as Northern California, surfers resorted to desperate means to keep from freezing. Some even wore wool sweaters in the water. That changed in 1952 when Jack O'Neill, a San Francisco surfer, made the first wet suit by sewing a bodysuit together from neoprene, a material similar to rubber. A wet suit *(right)* works by allowing a thin layer of water into the suit, which is then trapped and warmed by the body. The colder the water, the thicker the suit the surfer wears.

● **BOARD:** The first surfboards were made from slabs of wood harvested from trees. In the early 20th century, surfers were still making their own boards, usually out of redwood. The boards measured roughly 10 feet long by 2 feet wide and weighed more than 100 pounds. This was the basic design until 1928, when surfer Tom Blake began making hollow boards. These were lighter (about 60 pounds) and more maneuverable. Blake soon added a fin to the board's bottom to aid in turning. He sold his boards to other surfers, which meant that for the first time they didn't have to make their own. Boards changed again in the 1950's, when fiberglass and plastic resin were laid over balsa, a very lightweight wood. In 1958, polyurethane foam replaced balsa, and the modern surfboard was born.

Boards continue to evolve and now come in a variety of shapes and sizes. They fall into three basic categories: longboards, shortboards, and hybrids.

A longboard has a rounded nose, measures from 8 to 12 feet long, and usually comes with one fin. Despite its size, it weighs 15 pounds or less. A longboard is more stable and buoyant than a shortboard and is propelled easily on smaller waves. Beginners often learn to surf on a longboard. A shortboard can be 5½ feet or longer and has a different shape than a longboard. It has a narrow, pointed nose and usually comes with three fins. A shortboard is faster and more maneuverable than a longboard. A hybrid combines elements of a longboard and a shortboard. It is shorter than a longboard (from 6' 6" to 7' 6" in length) but it's as maneuverable as a shortboard.

● **LEASH:** All boards are now equipped with leashes, which first appeared regularly in the 1970's. Early surfers had to abandon their boards during a wipeout and swim to shore to retrieve them before paddling out again. Leashes save the hassle of chasing boards, allowing surfers to catch more waves. Today's leashes are fixed to a leash cup on the top rear of the surfboard and attach to the ankle with a Velcro strap.

BODY GLOVE

AERIAL REVERSE 360

KAREN WILSON/TOSTEE.COM

BRUCE IRONS

He may be three-time world champ And Irons's little brother, but Bruce Irons knows how to go big. The tour pro from Kaua Hawaii, is one of the most thrilling surfers watch when he goes airborne. His mos spectacular move was the aerial reverse 36 he pulled when he won the 2005 Mr. Price Pr at Jeffreys Bay in South Africa. Irons charges hard and flies high. He even crashes spectacularly. His personal highlight reel, *The Bruce Movie*, was released in 2005. It was named Video of the Year and earned him Bes Performance by a Male in the 2005 *Surfer* Poll and Video Awards.

┌TIME LINE├

PRE-1778

Polynesians in Tahiti, Hawaii, and other South Pacific islands ride through the thundering surf on planks from trees.

1778 British sea captain James

Cook arrives in Hawaii on the ship *Resolution*. His crew returns to Europe with tales of natives riding the waves.

1912 Duke Kahanamoku, a Waikiki surfer and

swimmer, wins a gold medal in the 100-meter freestyle at the Olympics. After the Games, he travels the world, performing surfing demonstrations.

Duke Kahanamoku

AP

< LEGEND >
KELLY SLATER

Kelly Slater is the most famous surfer in the world — and for good reason. He is the best to ever step on a board. During the 1990's, Slater took the ASP Tour by storm. He changed competitive surfing forever by introducing aerials and other tricks into every wave. The native of Cocoa Beach, Florida, honed his moves on the East Coast and won four national amateur championships. He turned pro at age 18 in 1990. Using a combination of creativity and burning competitive drive, Slater won his first world championship in 1992. After that, he dabbled in acting, joining the cast of the hit television show, *Baywatch*. Slater's ranking fell to sixth in the world in 1993, and other surfers made fun of his Hollywood act. The setback turned out to be a wake-up call. Slater quit TV and refocused his attention on surfing. Riding waves like no one before, he carved more maneuvers and linked more aerials. The result was five world championship titles in a row (1994-98). By then, Slater was 26 and bored, so he retired in 1999. He returned to the world tour in 2002, but victories didn't come as easily as before. Slater finished ninth, second, and third on the tour his first three years back. But, in 2005, he showed he still had the stuff as he battled to win his seventh world title at age 33.

NATHAN SMITH

FAST FACT
The lineup is the place where surfers wait in the water for waves.

1928 Tom Blake of the United States wins the Pacific Coast Surf Riding Championships at Corona Del Mar, California. He uses a hollow board that weighs less than 100 pounds, inspiring others to copy his design.

1953 *The San Francisco Chronicle* publishes a photo of Buzzy Trent, Woody Brown, and George Downing riding a massive wave at Makaha on the west coast of Oahu, Hawaii. The photo inspires legions of surfing pilgrims to head to Hawaii.

1958 Surfer and board manufacturer Hobie Alter begins large-scale production of foam-based surfboards with partner Gordon "Grubby" Clark in Dana Point, California. Hobie Surfboards soon makes 200 boards per week using materials that lay the foundation for today's designs.

COURTESY OF HOBIE

THE BASIC TRICKS

BOTTOM TURN▶

The bottom turn is the move a surfer masters after learning how to stand on the board and cruise down the face of a wave. It means turning in the direction of the breaking wave. On bigger, faster waves, a bottom turn is essential before the wave crashes on the surfer's head.

SCOTT NEEDHAM

◀ CUTBACK

After making a bottom turn, the surfer reverses direction and heads back to the top of the breaking wave. This gives the surfer a longer ride. The cutback is an intermediate move, but true masters pull it off with style and power.

SCOTT NEEDHAM

GETTING BARRELED▶

This move, also called "getting tubed," requires expert surfing skills and larger, steeper waves that break over a shallow reef or sandbar. Those conditions create a hollow tube or barrel inside the wave. A surfer drops in on the wave as late as possible and then barely gets under the lip of the wave before it breaks. The surfer then remains inside the barrel for a wet and wild ride, getting out before the wave crashes and wipes him out.

NATHAN SMITH

TIME LINE

1959 *Gidget*, a movie about a girl surfer and her friends in Malibu, California, is released. The film introduces surfing to people from coast to coast. Demand for surfboards skyrockets.

1961 Phil Edwards of the United States is the first surfer to drop in and ride the barrel of a wave at Banzai Pipeline on the North Shore of Oahu, Hawaii.

1966 Filmmaker Bruce Brown releases *The Endless Summer*, about two young surfers who travel the globe in search of the perfect wave. The movie is considered a classic and, to some, the greatest surfing movie of all time.

The Endless Summer
A FILM BY BRUCE BROWN

Laird Hamilton had already wowed the surfing world by being towed into 50-foot waves as if he were dropping in on 6-footers on an average day. But on August 17, 2000, Hamilton did the impossible when he took off on what many believe to be the heaviest wave ever ridden, in Teahupoo, Tahiti.

Even the most confident surfers considered the ride a suicide mission. The waves at Teahupoo are as thick as they are tall and break extremely quickly, creating a violent, foaming tube. The massive wave curled over Hamilton as he crouched low. One false move would have turned him into fish food on the razor-sharp reef below. After cruising to safety, Hamilton was so moved by the experience that he broke down and cried.

Teahupoo had been a stop on the pro tour, but some top surfers were scared to ride there even when the waves were smaller. Hamilton and his epic ride helped lead the way through the big, nasty barrel.

Laird Hamilton is the world's best monster-wave surfer.

ROBERT BROWN

F[A]S[T] FACT

A *grommet* is a young surfer who is respected but whose status is low in the lineup. The word is believed to be a variation of the term *gremlin*.

1969 Legendary big-wave pioneer Greg Noll of the United States rides a 30-foot monster at Makaha in Oahu. For nearly 30 years, this stood as the biggest wave ever ridden.

1975 Jeff Clark of the United States becomes the first surfer to ride Maverick's, a treacherous big-wave spot in Northern California.

Maverick's

ARIC CRABB/AP

1976 Surfers Fred Hemmings and Randy Rarick of the United States create International Professional Surfers, the first world tour with points awarded at each contest.

1979 Mark Richards of Australia wins the first of his four consecutive world titles.

<UP-AND-COMER>
DANE REYNOLDS

The future of men's surfing is a 20-year-old from Long Beach, California. Dane Reynolds's talent as a trick surfer was recognized early at the National Scholastic Surfing Association's Western Championships. He won the event as a 16-year-old in 2001 and has continued to climb the sport's ranks. Reynolds was the youngest surfer in the field at the 2003, 2004, and 2005 X Games. He competed for the West team. Even though the East won each time, Reynolds awed the crowd with his aerials. In 2004, he beat reigning pro tour champ Andy Irons in a head-to-head heat during a competition at Lower Trestles, in San Clemente, California. *Surfer* magazine ranked him Number 1 in its annual Hot 100 for 2005.

ASPWORLDTOUR.COM/TOSTEE

⊢TIME LINE⊢

1985 Tom Curren of California becomes the first non-Australian to win a world championship. He wins again the following year and in 1990.

PIERRE TOSTEE/GETTY IMAGES

Tom Curren

1992 Rookie Kelly Slater of Cocoa Beach, Florida, wins the world championship. He wins a record five more titles over the next six years before temporarily retiring in 1999.

1994 Lisa Andersen of the United States wins the first of four consecutive women's world titles.

GROUNDBREAKING TRICK
AERIALS

MATT KECHELE

Matt Kechele grew up an avid surfer and skateboarder in Cocoa Beach, Florida, during the 1970's. Another Florida skateboarder named Alan Gelfand had a great influence on Kechele's surfing. Gelfand had recently invented a no-handed aerial called the "ollie." Kechele began pulling similar no-handed aerials on waves at the world-famous break at Sebastian Inlet. His style was ahead of its time and didn't get good marks from judges during contests. But Kechele stuck with his airs during free-surfing sessions. Eventually, he spotted a young kid ripping the waves at Cocoa Beach. That kid was Kelly Slater, and Kechele's style would have a huge effect on the future world champion. Kechele mentored Slater on surf trips around the East Coast, teaching him contest strategy. By age 16, Slater would step out on his own and dominate competitive surfing for the next 10 years and beyond, using the stylish aerials pioneered by Kechele.

1998 Ken Bradshaw of the United States rides a record 85-foot-high wave at a reef called Outside Log Cabins on the North Shore of Oahu.

2003 Layne Beachley of Australia wins her record sixth straight women's world championship.

2004 Andy Irons of the United States wins his third straight world title.

2005 Kelly Slater wins his record seventh world title after returning in 2002 from retirement. Chelsea Georgeson of Australia wins the women's world championship.

Kelly Slater

PIERRE TOSTEE

TOP 10 ATHLETES

1 **KELLY SLATER**, born February 11, 1972, in Cocoa Beach, Florida. Slater has won a record seven world championships and is the greatest competition and free surfer in the sport. He won his first world title as a 21-year-old rookie. His style and aggression changed competitive surfing. Slater retired from the pro tour for three years before returning in 2002 and winning another title in 2005.

Kelly Slater

NATHAN SMITH

2 **ANDY IRONS**, born July 24, 1978, in Kauai, Hawaii. Irons won world championships from 2002 through 2004. He burst onto the surfing scene as a 17-year-old in 1996, when he outsurfed veterans Derek Ho and Shane Beschen in the final of the HIC Pipeline Pro event. Irons and his younger brother, Bruce, also a top pro, were raised on some of the world's best surf and pushed each other to excel as kids.

3 **LAIRD HAMILTON**, born March 2, 1964, in San Francisco, California. It's hard to measure Hamilton's success because he doesn't compete — instead, measure it by the waves he rides. Hamilton goes after only the biggest waves, regularly riding 50-foot-plus monsters at places that can only be reached by personal watercraft. Hamilton pioneered the tow-in surfing movement. He rides massive tow-in waves with a stylish flow and is always looking for the next big set on the horizon. Although he'll never win a world tour title, many consider him the greatest surfer ever.

Joel Parkinson

ASPWORLDTOUR.COM/TOSTEE

4 **MICK FANNING**, born June 13, 1981, in Sydney, Australia. Considered one of the fastest surfers ever, Fanning finished fourth on the world tour in 2003, but missed most of 2004 with a hamstring injury. Known for his awesome talent and great sense of humor, Fanning returned in 2005 with a renewed dedication to surfing. He won two of the first five events of the season and finished fourth in the final standings.

5 **JOEL PARKINSON**, born April 10, 1981, in Nambour, Australia. The mellow Australian turned pro in 2001 and finished 21st on the World Championship Tour. He has since finished second (2002) and fifth (2004) on the tour. His surfing style looks casual but quickly becomes explosive when he's charging for a wave.

6 C.J. HOBGOOD, born July 6, 1979, in Melbourne, Florida. Hobgood learned to surf in the same Central Florida breaks as Kelly Slater. He followed the legend to the top with a similar arsenal of tricks. Hobgood was ASP Rookie of the Year in 1999, the year a bored and burned-out Slater retired. With Slater out of the picture, Hobgood won the world championship in 2001 and remains a threat for another title. His twin brother, Damien, rips on the world tour, too.

Taj Burrow

7 TAJ BURROW, born June 2, 1978, in Busselton, Australia. Burrow was raised in Western Australia among some of the country's best point breaks and reefs. He won his first contest at age 9 — in the competition's under-18 division. Burrow went on to win just about every major award in junior surfing, including Young Australian Sportsperson of the Year. His pro career began the same way. He was named ASP Rookie of the Year in 1998 and finished second in the world tour standings to champ Mark Occhilupo in 1999.

8 CORY LOPEZ, born March 21, 1977, in Indian Rocks Beach, Florida. Lopez is another Florida ripper and part of another brother combo: Shea, his older brother, is also an ASP standout. Cory qualified for the ASP World Tour in 1998 and finished third in the final standings in 2001. He distinguished himself as fast, fearless, and capable of any trick. He's also a consistent Top 5 threat year after year.

Sofia Mulanovich

9 SOFIA MULANOVICH, born June 24, 1983, in Lima, Peru. In 2004, Mulanovich became the first South American, man or woman, to win a world championship. She halted Layne Beachley's streak of six world titles. Mulanovich finished second to Chelsea Georgeson in 2005.

10 LAYNE BEACHLEY, born May 24, 1972, in Sydney, Australia. Beachley has the perfect name for surfing. She ruled the women's pro tour the same way that Kelly Slater dominated the men's tour. From 1998 to 2003, she won the world tour championship a record six straight times. Beachley is also one of the few women to excel at big-wave surfing.

ASSOCIATION OF SURFING PROFESSIONALS (ASP) CHAMPIONS

MEN

YEAR	
2005	Kelly Slater, U.S.
2004	Andy Irons, U.S.
2003	Andy Irons, U.S.
2002	Andy Irons, U.S.
2001	C.J. Hobgood, U.S.
2000	Sunny Garcia, U.S.
1999	Mark Occhilupo, Australia
1998	Kelly Slater, U.S.
1997	Kelly Slater, U.S.
1996	Kelly Slater, U.S.
1995	Kelly Slater, U.S.
1994	Kelly Slater, U.S.
1993	Derek Ho, U.S.
1992	Kelly Slater, U.S.
1991	Damien Hardman, Australia
1990	Tom Curren, U.S.
1989	Martin Potter, Great Britain
1988	Barton Lynch, Australia
1987	Damien Hardman, Australia
1986	Tom Curren, U.S.
1985	Tom Curren, U.S.
1984	Tom Carroll, Australia
1983	Tom Carroll, Australia
1982	Mark Richards, Australia
1981	Mark Richards, Australia
1980	Mark Richards, Australia
1979	Mark Richards, Australia
1978	Wayne Bartholomew, Australia
1977	Shaun Tomson, South Africa
1976	Peter Townend, Australia

WOMEN

YEAR	
2005	Chelsea Georgeson, Australia
2004	Sofia Mulanovich, Peru
2003	Layne Beachley, Australia
2002	Layne Beachley, Australia
2001	Layne Beachley, Australia
2000	Layne Beachley, Australia
1999	Layne Beachley, Australia
1998	Layne Beachley, Australia
1997	Lisa Andersen, U.S.
1996	Lisa Andersen, U.S.
1995	Lisa Andersen, U.S.
1994	Lisa Andersen, U.S.
1993	Pauline Menczer, Australia
1992	Wendy Botha, Australia
1991	Wendy Botha, Australia
1990	Pam Burridge, Australia
1989	Wendy Botha, Australia
1988	Frieda Zamba, U.S.
1987	Wendy Botha, South Africa
1986	Frieda Zamba, U.S.
1985	Frieda Zamba, U.S.
1984	Frieda Zamba, U.S.
1983	Kim Mearig, U.S.
1982	Debbie Beacham, U.S.
1981	Margo Oberg, U.S.
1980	Margo Oberg, U.S.
1979	Lynne Boyer, U.S.
1978	Lynne Boyer, U.S.
1977	Margo Oberg, U.S.

YEAR	LONGBOARD
2005	Joel Tudor, U.S.
2004	Joel Tudor, U.S.
2003	Beau Young, Australia
2002	Colin McPhillips, U.S.
2001	Colin McPhillips, U.S.
2000	Beau Young, Australia
1999	Colin McPhillips, U.S.
1998	Joel Tudor, U.S.
1997	Dino Miranda, U.S.
1996	Bonga Perkins, U.S.
1995	Rusty Keaulana, U.S.
1994	Rusty Keaulana, U.S.
1993	Rusty Keaulana, U.S.
1992	Joey Hawkins, U.S.
1991	Martin McMillan, Australia
1990	Nat Young, Australia
1989	Nat Young, Australia
1988	Nat Young, Australia
1987	Stuart Entwistle, Australia
1986	Nat Young, Australia

X GAMES RESULTS

YEAR	GOLD	SILVER
2005	East Coast	West Coast
2004	East Coast	West Coast
2003	East Coast	West Coast

VANS TRIPLE CROWN OF SURFING CHAMPIONS

MEN

YEAR	
2005	Andy Irons, U.S.
2004	Sunny Garcia, U.S.
2003	Andy Irons, U.S.
2002	Andy Irons, U.S.
2001	Myles Padaca, U.S.
2000	Sunny Garcia, U.S.
1999	Sunny Garcia, U.S.
1998	Kelly Slater, U.S.
1997	Mike Rommelse, Australia
1996	Kaipo Jaquias, U.S.
1995	Kelly Slater, U.S.
1994	Sunny Garcia, U.S.
1993	Sunny Garcia, U.S.
1992	Sunny Garcia, U.S.
1991	Tom Carroll, Australia
1990	Derek Ho, U.S.
1989	Gary Elkerton, Australia
1988	Derek Ho, U.S.
1987	Gary Elkerton, Australia
1986	Derek Ho, U.S.
1985	Michael Ho, U.S.
1984	Derek Ho, U.S.
1983	Michael Ho, U.S.

WOMEN

YEAR	
2005	Chelsea Georgeson, Australia
2004	Chelsea Georgeson, Australia
2003	Keala Kennelly, U.S.
2002	Nerida Falconer, Australia
2001	Not held
2000	Heather Clarke, South Africa
1999	Trudy Todd, Australia
1998	Layne Beachley, Australia
1997	Layne Beachley, Australia

Two-time Vans Triple Crown champ Andy Irons

BO BRIDGES

1 TEAHUPOO, TAHITI. The type of wave found in Teahupoo (pronounced *cho-pu)* is considered the heaviest and deadliest in the world because of its thickness. It is the ultimate test of skill and courage for the world's best surfers. The wave is created when uninterrupted ocean swells suddenly surge upward on the coral reefs surrounding the island. It has been ridden regularly only for about 10 years and still has the reputation as the gnarliest wave in the world.

Teahupoo, Tahiti

2 BANZAI PIPELINE, HAWAII. The Banzai Pipeline is located on the North Shore of Oahu. Its perfect surf is created when the top of the wave curls over, resulting in a hollow tube that gutsy surfers can ride inside. A surfer emerges or the wave swallows him and his board and spits him out onto the razor-sharp reef a few feet below. The Pipeline breaks in the 10-foot range, but the outer reefs can produce even larger waves under the right circumstances.

3 WAIMEA BAY, HAWAII. Waimea is located on Oahu's North Shore and was the proving ground for early big-wave surfers during the 1950's. Massive ocean swells enter the bay and heave up on its lava shelf, producing waves topping 20 feet. Waimea is one of the easier big-wave spots in the world, but the initial drop is terrifying.

Waimea Bay, Hawaii

DONALD MIRALLE/GETTY IMAGES

4 JEFFREYS BAY, SOUTH AFRICA. J-Bay is located on a remote stretch of coast between the cities of Durban and Cape Town. The waves there are regarded as among the world's best due to their size and shape. The highlight is the section of the break called Supertubes, which produces waves as long as 200 yards.

5 TRESTLES, SAN CLEMENTE, CALIFORNIA. Named for the trestles, or framework, that support the railroad tracks near the shore, this remote spot in Southern California has four distinct breaks. The two worth noting are Lowers and Uppers. The best is Lowers, a south-facing bay that attracts the world's best surfers. Uppers is less congested and breaks from both directions, so it is more consistent.

6 GOLD COAST, AUSTRALIA. The Aussies call it "Goldie." Its 30 miles of coast near Brisbane has produced some of the sport's best surfers, including legends Peter Townend and Wayne "Rabbit" Bartholomew and current stars Joel Parkinson and Mick Fanning. Like the gold in its name, it is precious and desired by many. Therefore, the lineup is always crowded. Warm air and water temperatures make it a year-round destination.

Gold Coast, Australia

ASPWORLDTOUR.COM/TOSTEE

7 BELLS BEACH, AUSTRALIA. Located along the Surf Coast of Victoria, Bells rings when southern storms passing Australia kick up big waves on the rock reef. The first modern pro surfing event was held here in 1961, and the legend of Bells has grown ever since.

8 MAKAHA POINT, HAWAII. Located on the west side of the island of Oahu, Makaha Point is the birthplace of big-wave surfing. In 1969, legendary big-wave rider Greg Noll survived a ride on a 30-footer here. Makaha consists of four sections, and waves can top 10 feet.

9 SEBASTIAN INLET, FLORIDA. The East Coast usually ranks far behind Hawaii, Australia, and California as a surfing destination. Sebastian is the exception. A jetty on the Central Florida Coast produces a series of high-performance waves, ideal for tricks like aerials, which were invented here in 1979 by local Matt Kechele. Sebastian has also been a launching point for some of surfing's top pros, such as Kelly Slater, and the Hobgood and Lopez brothers.

10 MAVERICK'S, HALF MOON BAY, CALIFORNIA. This legendary big-wave spot between San Francisco and Santa Cruz can produce 50-foot monsters. During such conditions, it tests the world's best big-wave riders. Local Jeff Clark first rode Maverick's in 1975, and had it to himself for years because no one else dared to try it. Then in 1990, word leaked out and lured big-wave surfers worldwide. But it has yet to be tamed. In 1994, big-wave master Mark Foo of Hawaii died after a wipeout here.

Maverick's, Half Moon Bay, California

SCOTT WINER/A-FRAME

CHAPTER 9

WAKEBOARDING

Watch a wakeboarder pull tricks, and you'll see the sport's roots in waterskiing, surfing, snowboarding, and skateboarding.

Phillip Soven won his first X Games gold medal at age 15.

W akeboarding's roots can be traced back to 1985. That's when two surfers in separate parts of the United States came up with the same idea: Build shorter boards that riders can stand on to carve the waves ("the wake") created by a motorboat. The surfers' creation evolved into what is now called wakeboarding. More than 20 years later, the sport — which has elements of waterskiing, surfing, skateboarding, and snowboarding — has carved its own identity.

Dallas Friday is the most successful female wakeboarder.

BILL DOSTER

The Inventors
Tony Finn and Jimmy Redmon were the California surfers who designed and built the first wakeboards — or ski boards, as they were called. Finn, from San Diego, created the Skurfer, a cross between a water ski and a surfboard. Meanwhile, Redmon, who was attending college in landlocked Austin, Texas, built the Redline water ski board to ride the wakes made by boats in the area lakes. At first, both inventions allowed the rider to stand anywhere on the board because there were no straps or bindings holding the rider in place. But both Finn and Redmon added footstraps to their products, which enabled riders to get big air when they hit the wake.

A Better Board
Finn and Redmon shared a great idea, but their designs were flawed. Their boards floated like surfboards, making it difficult to stand on them from a stopped position. The problem was corrected in 1990, when Herb O'Brien created his Hyperlite model board. O'Brien, a water ski manufacturer, made his board from materials that kept it submerged until the boat towing the rider began picking up speed. That made the board more stable and easier for a rider to stand on, even in deep water. The sport soon began to take off.

The Sport Takes Shape
Wakeboarding became an organized sport in 1989, when Redmon created the World Wakeboard Association, in Orlando, Florida. As the sport's international governing body, it established rules and competition formats. In 1992, the first pro wakeboard events were held. At the time, wakeboarding was still heavily influenced by waterskiing, so the sports' contests were similar. Results were based on points earned for tricks done during a required freestyle session.

Parks Bonifay
is a five-time
Pro Wakeboarding
Tour champion.

In 1993, Redmon and Finn joined forces to start a board company called Wake Tech. With their design influence and a roster of phenomenal riders, Wake Tech literally reshaped wakeboarding. Previous boards were designed like surfboards, with an obvious tip and tail. One of Wake Tech's innovations was to create a board with a tip on each end. The symmetrical, or balanced, shape allowed the rider to stand forward or backward and attempt more difficult tricks.

Wakeboarding's Future

Competition continued to evolve, too. In 2000, sliders (rails) and jump ramps were added to pro courses. Judging became more subjective: A rider was evaluated on his overall flow, as well as his use of the wake, sliders, and ramps. Wakeboarding even produced another discipline — wakeskating — in which riders pull skateboard-style tricks on boards without straps or bindings. Wakeskating's first pro tour began in 2003.

Today, wakeboarding and wakeskating have grown to include approximately 2.7 million riders worldwide. But the sports continue to look to the future as riders strive to create bigger, more complicated tricks.

FAST FACT

When the boat takes a wide turn and approaches the old wake at a 90-degree angle, the new and old wakes meet. The waves created can be twice as big. This is called a "double up."

Aaron Rathy was an accomplished amateur water-skier in Canada but quit the sport in 2004 to try wakeboarding. Eight months later, the 17-year-old won two gold medals at the Canadian Wakeboarding Championships. Rathy brings an aggressive style to wakeboarding — and wakeskating — that comes from his background as a skateboarder and snowboarder. He made his pro debut at Wakestock 2005, the world's largest wakeboarding and wakeskating event, held in Toronto Islands, Ontario, Canada. The native of Nanaimo, British Columbia, won Best Trick on a wakeskate and finished second in the wakeboard Railslide event.

GARRETT CORTESE

INNOVATOR
THOMAS HORRELL

During the mid-1990's, Thomas Horrell, now 28 years old, was a top pro wakeboarder with a polished style. Although he finished fifth in the pro tour standings in 1996, he had become less interested in the pro wakeboarding scene. He and a few other riders had begun experimenting with a variation of wakeboarding called wakeskating. They would get towed behind boats on skateboard decks with no footstraps or bindings and pull tricks off the wake. At first, it was just an activity wakeboarders fooled around with in their spare time. But Horrell was excited by the possibilities. He quit the pro tour and dedicated himself to wakeskating. Horrell pursued progressive tricks and pioneered better equipment through his wakeskating company, Cassette. His talent on the water and his commitment to the sport have led to its rapid growth. Wakeskating has gotten so popular that a pro tour

ME MURRAY/RED BULL

Before the sport was officially known as wakeboarding, it was called skiboarding, the ugly stepchild of waterskiing. Then, in 1993, along came Wake Tech, a company dedicated to skiboarding. Soon after forming a roster of riders with backgrounds in surfing, skateboarding, and snowboarding, Wake Tech carved out a new sport with its own identity: wakeboarding.

Wake Tech built its reputation on two phenomenal riders, Scott Byerly and Erik "Gator" Lutgert. Byerly pulled new tricks with a smooth style that others have since strived to imitate, and Lutgert simply went huge. Together, they made waves in the waterskiing community with their long hair and radical riding.

Innovations in Wake Tech's board design helped push the pair to greater achievements. By 1994, the company had designed a new type of twin-tip board that let riders do tricks backward or forward. On the new boards, Byerly won the 1994 world championships and Lutgert placed second. Their riding demonstrated what was possible, making them representatives of the growing sport.

Wake Tech pushed Erik "Gator" Lutgert to greater heights.

COURTESY OF GATOR BOARDS

FAST FACT

Dallas Friday of Orlando, Florida, was a competitive gymnast for five years before trying wakeboarding at age 12. She turned pro at age 13 after winning the silver medal at the 2000 X Games.

TIME LINE

1985 Tony Finn creates the Skurfer and Jimmy Redmon creates the Redline water ski board. Both designs lead to the first wakeboard.

COURTESY OF LIQUID FORCE

Tony Finn

1989 The World Wakeboard Association is founded, leading to rules and competition formats for the new sport.

1990 The Hyperlite board is created, allowing for deep-water starts. It is the first true wakeboard.

Hyperlite boa

THE 1080

PARKS BONIFAY

In 1999, 18-year-old Parks Bonifay pulled the first 1080-degree spin (three full rotations) to be captured on film. No one has accomplished the trick since — or at least it's never been proven with photos. The trick is considered the toughest to do and intimidates even the best riders. The 1080 requires passing the towrope's handle so many times that many riders eventually lose their grip.

1992 The first pro wakeboard
nts are held, leading to
Pro Wakeboard Tour.
n Shapiro of the United
tes wins the tour's first
mpionship, then repeats
993.

1994 Wake Tech introduces its Flight
69 twin tip symmetrical board. It
sets the standard for board
design today, allowing boarders
to ride "switch stance" (backward
or forward).

1995 Darin Shapiro
wins his fourth straight
Pro Wakeboard Tour
title.

Darin Shapiro

THE BASIC TRICKS

SURFACE 180▶

The rider turns the board 180 degrees while skimming along the water, so that his back foot is now forward. This is one of the first tricks most wakeboarders learn.

CHRISTOF KOEPSEL/BONGARTS/GETTY IMAGES

PRESTON MACK

The rider digs the board's heelside edge hard into the water and forces it to turn 90 degrees. Leaning away from the boat causes a big spray of water, which looks cool but makes sliding slightly bumpy.

WAKE-TO-WAKE BACKSIDE AIR▶

Crossing both wakes requires big air. The rider approaches the wake with the heelside edge dug in and hits the top of the wake at top speed, with no slack in the towrope. Landing this move guarantees a giant leap from beginner to intermediate status.

JOEY MEDDOCK

TIME LINE

1996 The X Games adds wakeboarding to its program. At age 14, Parks Bonifay of the United States wins the first gold medal.

1999 Parks Bonifay lands the first – and so far only – 1080 spin (three rotations) to be captured on film.

BILL DOSTER

Parks Bonifay

2000 Darin Shapiro wins his record sixth Pro Wakeboard Tour title. The Pro Wakeboar Tour adds sliders and ramps to its format. Tara Hamilto the United States wins her third women's Pro Wakeboa Tour title.

2001 Dallas Friday, age 14, wins gold medals at the X Games and Gravity Games.

GROUNDBREAKING TRICK
KICKFLIP ON A WAKESKATE

THOMAS HORRELL

Wakeskates were inspired by skateboards and first appeared in the mid-1990's. Wakeskates were cool, but the best tricks were considered intermediate by skateboard standards and too hard for beginners to attempt. The tricks were also unimpressive compared to the big air of wakeboarding. Many people dismissed wakeskating as second-rate. Then in 1999, Thomas Horrell nailed a basic kickflip on a wakeskate during the filming of the video, *Boardumb*. Suddenly, the possibilities of trick progression grew and wakeskating gained more respect. The result: Since 2002, the number of pro wakeskaters has grown from approximately 20 riders to 100.

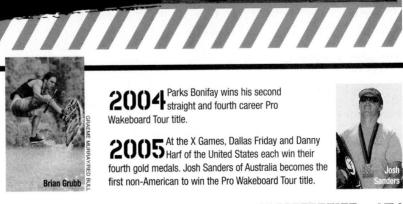

2003
akeskating gets its
vn pro tour. Brian
ubb of the United
ates wins the first
ampionship.

Brian Grubb

GRAEME MURRAY/RED BULL

2004
Parks Bonifay wins his second straight and fourth career Pro Wakeboard Tour title.

2005
At the X Games, Dallas Friday and Danny Harf of the United States each win their fourth gold medals. Josh Sanders of Australia becomes the first non-American to win the Pro Wakeboard Tour title.

Josh
Sanders

MIKE ISLER/MOON SMI

NECESSARY OBJECTS

- **WAKEBOARD/WAKESKATE:** A good wakeboard *(right)* balances pop and rideability. Pop is the amount of spring a rider gets when he pushes off the wake with his legs. Wider boards provide more pop, but they are tough to turn and are slower than narrower boards. Most boards are 15" to 17 ½" wide and 47" to 56" long. Shorter boards are less stable in starts and turns, so longer boards are better for beginners. Wakeboards are made of a foam core surrounded by fiberglass, graphite, or a combination of both (called composite). Wakeskates range from 15" to 17 ½" wide and from 38" to 45" long. They are made of wood or composite. Foam or grip tape tops the surface to give the rider traction.

- **TOWROPE:** A rider is just a pylon or a buoy floating in the water without a towrope *(left)*. All towropes are the same, and should not stretch. Stretchy ropes act as a bungee cord and would whip the rider around too much.

- **BOAT:** Any motorboat *(below)* strong enough to pull a boarder will do, and the Pro Wakeboard Tour even uses personal watercraft to pull riders. But all boats are not created equal. Adding weight to the boat's frame, or hull, sinks it deeper, which creates a bigger wake and, in turn, bigger air. Before recent innovations, one way to create weight, or ballast, was to add concrete or lead to the hull. Wake boats now have switches on the dashboard that load water into concealed containers and drain it as needed.

FAST FACT

Parks Bonifay set the Guinness World Record for being the youngest person to water-ski. He was six months old when his dad strapped him into training skis.

‹ LEGEND ›
DARIN SHAPIRO

In the early days of wakeboarding, Darin Shapiro was way ahead of the competition. At 5' 4", the compact rider was expected to win every contest — and he usually lived up to those expectations. Shapiro soared high and racked up an impressive list of accomplishments: six Pro Wakeboard Tour championships, including the first four from 1992 through 1995. Some of his other firsts include appearing on the cover of the debut issue of *Wakeboarding* magazine in 1993, and pulling the first double front flip during competition in 1997. Throughout his stellar career, Shapiro also won four world wakeboarding titles, and three gold medals and two silver medals at the X Games. He's now 32 years old, and his best days are in his wake, but Shapiro's standard of dominance remains.

TONY SMITH

‹ UP–AND–COMER ›
KEVIN HENSHAW

JOEY MEDDOCK

Another Canadian ripper, Kevin Henshaw, age 19, won the Junior X wakeboard series in 2004 and joined the Pro Wakeboard Tour in 2005. The Sidney, British Columbia, native finished 22nd on the tour but showed enormous potential, especially at Wakestock 2005. Henshaw placed fourth in the Expression Session against the world's best boarders.

TOP 10 ATHLETES

1 PARKS BONIFAY, wakeboarder, born September 30, 1981, in Winter Haven, Florida. Bonifay is the greatest free rider in the sport and the only rider to pull a 1080. He won his first Pro Wakeboard Tour championship at age 14 and has won four more (1998, 2001, 2003, and 2004).

2 DANNY HARF, wakeboarder, born October 15, 1984, in Visalia, California. Harf, age 21, is just entering his prime. He has already won four X Games gold medals (2001-03, 2005) and placed second on the Pro Wakeboarding Tour in 2004.

3 JOSH SANDERS, wakeboarder, born November 8, 1981, in Wollongong, Australia. Sanders became the first non-American to win the Pro Wakeboard Tour, in 2005.

Josh Sanders

4 DANIEL WATKINS, wakeboarder, born December 31, 1976, in Melbourne, Australia. The Australian vet won bronze at the 2003 X Games. He placed third on the pro tour in 2003 and 2004 and finished second in 2005.

Daniel Watkins

5 DALLAS FRIDAY, wakeboarder, born September 6, 1986, in Orlando, Florida. Friday is the sport's best female wakeboarder. At age 19, she has already won three world championships and a women's wakeboarding record six X Games medals.

BILL DOSTER

6 PHILLIP "FROGGY" SOVEN, wakeboarder, born June 4, 1989, in Longwood, Florida. The Longwood, Florida, native will likely be the dominant rider of the next 10 years. He joined the pro tour as an 11-year-old in 2001 and won X Games gold in 2004.

7 BRETT EISENHAUER, wakeboarder, born October 20, 1976, in Wagga Wagga, Australia. The consistent Australian finished fourth on the Pro Wakeboard Tour in 2001 and 2003 and third in 2005.

8 ANDREW ADKISON, wakeboarder, born April 8, 1982, in Chattanooga, Tennessee. Adkison was the Pro Wakeboard Tour Rookie of the Year in 2002 and the world champion in 2004.

9 BRIAN GRUBB, wakeskater, born July 31, 1980, in Orlando, Florida. Grubb won his first Pro Wakeskate Tour title in 2003 and finished third in 2005.

10 AARON REED, wakeskater, born September 25, 1981, in Stuart, Florida. Reed has become one of the leaders of the sport's progression with his mastery of lip-style skate tricks.

Brett Eisenhauer

TONY ASHBY/AFP/GETTY IMAGES

Aaron Reed

GRAEME MURRAY/RED BULL

X GAMES RESULTS

MEN

YEAR	GOLD	SILVER	BRONZE
2005	Danny Harf, U.S.	Phillip Soven, U.S.	Josh Sanders, U.S.
2004	Phillip Soven, U.S.	Chad Sharpe, Canada	Parks Bonifay, U.S.
2003	Danny Harf, U.S.	Parks Bonifay, U.S.	Daniel Watkins, U.S.
2002	Danny Harf, U.S.	Darin Shapiro, U.S.	Shaun Murray, U.S.
2001	Danny Harf, U.S.	Darin Shapiro, U.S.	Erik Ruck, U.S.
2000	Darin Shapiro, U.S.	Shaun Murray, U.S.	Shane Bonifay, U.S.
1999	Parks Bonifay, U.S.	Darin Shapiro, U.S.	Brannan Johnson, U.S.
1998	Darin Shapiro, U.S.	Shaun Murray, U.S.	Zane Schwenk, U.S.
1997	Jeremy Kovak, Canada	Darin Shapiro, U.S.	Parks Bonifay, U.S.
1996	Parks Bonifay, U.S.	Jeremy Kovak, Canada	Scott Byerly, U.S.

WOMEN

YEAR	GOLD	SILVER	BRONZE
2005	Dallas Friday, U.S.	Emily Copeland-Durham, U.S.	Tara Hamilton, U.S.
2004	Dallas Friday, U.S.	Tara Hamilton, U.S.	Maeghan Major, U.S.
2003	Dallas Friday, U.S.	Melissa Marquardt, U.S.	Emily Copeland-Durham, U.S.
2002	Emily Copeland, U.S.	Dallas Friday, U.S.	Leslie Kent, U.S.
2001	Dallas Friday, U.S.	Emily Copeland, U.S.	Tara Hamilton, U.S.
2000	Tara Hamilton, U.S.	Dallas Friday, U.S.	Maeghan Major, U.S.
1999	Maeghan Major, U.S.	Emily Copeland, U.S.	Andrea Gaytan, Mexico
1998	Andrea Gaytan, Mexico	Dana Preble, U.S.	Tara Hamilton, U.S.
1997	Tara Hamilton, U.S.	Andrea Gaytan, Mexico	Jaime Necrason, U.S.

Danny Harf

DOM COOLEY/SHAZAMM/ESPN IMAGES

GRAVITY GAMES RESULTS

MEN

YEAR	GOLD	SILVER	BRONZE
2005	Phillip Soven, U.S.	Daniel Watkins, Australia	Rusty Malinoski, Canada
2004	Trevor Hansen, U.S.	Andrew Adkison, U.S.	Brett Eisenhauer, Australia
2003	Parks Bonifay, U.S.	Shane Bonifay, U.S.	Brett Eisenhauer, Australia
2002	Mark Kenney, U.S.	Danny Harf, U.S.	Darin Shapiro, U.S.
2001	Darin Shapiro, U.S.	Parks Bonifay, U.S.	Daniel Watkins, Australia
2000	Parks Bonifay, U.S.	Darin Shapiro, U.S.	Ryan Wynne, U.S.
1999	Shaun Murray, U.S.	Parks Bonifay, U.S.	Rob Struharik, U.S

WOMEN

YEAR	GOLD	SILVER	BRONZE
2005	Emily Copeland-Durham, U.S.	Lauren Loe, U.S.	Dallas Friday, U.S.
2004	Dallas Friday, U.S.	Emily Copeland-Durham, U.S.	Lauren Loe, U.S.
2003	Emily Copeland-Durham, U.S.	Tara Hamilton, U.S.	Leslie Kent, U.S.
2002	Emily Copeland, U.S.	Melissa Marquardt, U.S.	Dallas Friday, U.S.
2001	Dallas Friday, U.S.	Tara Hamilton, U.S.	Christy Smith, U.S.
2000	Maeghan Major, U.S.	Tara Hamilton, U.S.	Lauren Loe, U.S.
1999	Andrea Gaytan, Mexico	Tara Hamilton, U.S.	Christy Smith, U.S.

PRO WAKEBOARD TOUR CHAMPIONS

MEN

YEAR	
2005	Josh Sanders, Australia
2004	Parks Bonifay, U.S.
2003	Parks Bonifay, U.S.
2002	Erik Ruck, U.S.
2001	Parks Bonifay, U.S.
2000	Darin Shapiro, U.S.
1999	Shaun Murray, U.S.
1998	Parks Bonifay, U.S.
1997	Darin Shapiro, U.S.
1996	Parks Bonifay, U.S.
1995	Darin Shapiro, U.S.
1994	Darin Shapiro, U.S.
1993	Darin Shapiro, U.S.
1992	Darin Shapiro, U.S.

WOMEN

YEAR	
2005	Dallas Friday, U.S.
2004	Dallas Friday and Emily Copeland-Durham, U.S.
2003	Dallas Friday, U.S.
2002	N/A
2001	Emily Copeland, U.S.
2000	Tara Hamilton, U.S.
1999	Emily Copeland, U.S.
1998	Tara Hamilton, U.S.
1997	Tara Hamilton, U.S.

PRO WAKESKATE TOUR CHAMPIONS

YEAR	
2005	Brandon Thomas, U.S.
2004	Phillip Basino, U.S.
2003	Brian Grubb, U.S.

NATIONAL WAKEBOARD CHAMPIONS

MEN

YEAR	
2005	Danny Harf
2004	Tino Santori
2003	Danny Harf
2002	Shawn Weston
2001	Parks Bonifay
2000	Shawn Weston
1999	Shaun Murray
1998	Ryan Siebring
1997	Parks Bonifay

WOMEN

YEAR	
2005	Dallas Friday
2004	Dallas Friday
2003	Dallas Friday
2002	Dallas Friday
2001	Emily Copeland
2000	Maeghan Major
1999	Tara Hamilton
1998	Tara Hamilton

NATIONAL WAKESKATE CHAMPIONS

YEAR	
2005	Phillip Basino
2004	Steve Schoenhals
2003	Brian Grubb

WAKEBOARD WORLD CHAMPIONS

MEN

YEAR	
2005	Phillip Soven, U.S.
2004	Andrew Adkison, U.S.
2003	Shaun Murray, U.S.
2002	Erik Ruck, U.S.
2001	Darin Shapiro, U.S.
2000	Shaun Murray, U.S.
1999	Darin Shapiro, U.S.
1998	Shaun Murray, U.S.
1997	Jeremy Kovak, Canada

WOMEN

YEAR	
2005	Emily Copeland-Durham, U.S.
2004	Dallas Friday, U.S.
2003	Dallas Friday, U.S.
2002	Tara Hamilton, U.S.
2001	Emily Copeland, U.S.
2000	Maeghan Major, U.S.
1999	Tara Hamilton, U.S.
1998	Tara Hamilton, U.S.
1997	Tara Hamilton, U.S.

WAKESKATE WORLD CHAMPIONS

YEAR	
2005	Brandon Thomas, U.S.
2004	George Daniels, U.S.
2003	Brian Grubb, U.S.

WAKEBOARD WORLD CUP CHAMPIONS

MEN

YEAR	
2005	Phillip Soven, U.S.
2004	Parks Bonifay, U.S.
2003	Darin Shapiro, U.S.
2002	Darin Shapiro, U.S.
2001	Parks Bonifay, U.S.
2000	Darin Shapiro, U.S.
1999	Brannan Johnson, U.S.
1998	Darin Shapiro, U.S.

WOMEN

YEAR	
2005	Emily Copeland-Durham, U.S.
2004	Dallas Friday, U.S.
2003	Dallas Friday, U.S.
2002	Emily Copeland, U.S.
2001	Dallas Friday, U.S.
2000	Maeghan Major, U.S.
1999	Tara Hamilton, U.S.
1998	Tara Hamilton, U.S.

TOP 10 PLACES TO RIDE

1 CENTRAL FLORIDA. There are hundreds of lakes to choose from within 30 miles of Orlando. The variety and volume make the area a wakeboarder's paradise.

Central Florida
TONY SMITH

2 LAKE POWELL, ARIZONA. Lake Powell is 186 miles long. It was created by the Glen Canyon Dam. The lake is located in the high desert and is surrounded by red rock walls, creating many canyons perfect for uninterrupted wakeboarding.

3 LAKE SHASTA, CALIFORNIA. In a mountainous region of Northern California, Lake Shasta is a sprawling body of water created by the Shasta Dam, which traps the waters of the Pit, McCloud, and Sacramento rivers. The Sacramento Arm portion of the lake is calm and best for wakeboarding.

Orlando Watersports Complex
COURTESY OF O.W.C.

4 ORLANDO WATERSPORTS COMPLEX, ORLANDO, FLORIDA. This is the premier wakeboarding and wakeskating facility in the world. It features a slider park with rails and a funbox with cables. Cables, not boats, pull riders of all skill levels, including many top pros who live nearby.

5 TEXAS SKI RANCH, NEW BRAUNFELS, TEXAS. Located halfway between San Antonio and Austin, the Texas Ski Ranch is a sprawling facility that features a skateboard park, climbing walls, and a motocross track. Wakeboarding facilities include a cable lake and a boat lake; each is equipped with kickers and sliders.

6 THE DELTA, SACRAMENTO, CALIFORNIA. The Delta is a tangle of tributaries fed by the San Joaquin and Sacramento rivers on their way to the Pacific Ocean. The area was popular with miners, trappers, and farmers during the 1800's, but wakeboarders rule in the 21st century.

7 LAKE OF THE OZARKS, MISSOURI. The Osage River was dammed in 1931 and the result was the 92-square-mile Lake of the Ozarks. It features plenty of coves for sheltered wakeboarding.

8 BULLARDS BAR, CALIFORNIA. Bullards Bar is a reservoir in Northern California that is surrounded by a national forest. It is a peaceful, uncrowded lake with warm water in summer and many sheltered rocky coves that are protected from the wind.

Bullards Bar
JOEY MEDDOCK

9 LAKE MEAD, LAS VEGAS, NEVADA. Lake Mead is an oasis of water in the deserts of Nevada and nearby Arizona. It was formed in 1935 after Hoover Dam was built along the Colorado River. Like Lake Powell in Arizona, Lake Mead's canyons provide shelter for nonstop wakeboarding.

10 CARLSBAD LAGOON, CARLSBAD, CALIFORNIA. The lagoon is a calm, flat lake in the midst of surf-crazed Southern California. It tends to be less crowded due to limited access.